THE COMPLETE JAMES BOND LIFESTYLE SEMINAR

PAUL KYRIAZI

THE COMPLETE
JAMES BOND LIFESTYLE SEMINAR.

Printed in the United States of America September 2002.

For information address:
Ronin Books
12335 Santa Monica Boulevard, FMB 116
Los Angeles, CA 90025.
Kyriazi@usa.net

www.BondLife.com
ISBN 0-9716183-0-5

Cover Design: Greg Pless
Editing: Sonny Culbertson
culbertsonny@hotmail.com
Designers: Gerry Serrano & Sonny Culbertson

Printed by Alonzo Printing Company
on recycled paper with soy-based ink.
alonzoprinting.com

Dedicated to George Lazenby,
who made my favorite Bond film.

Though Sean Connery is the best,
if I had to be Bond, I'd be Lazenby.

THE JAMES BOND LIFESTYLE SEMINAR

ACKNOWLEDGMENTS

Linda K, publicist extraordinaire, who encouraged me to get these techniques down on tape, and then on paper.

Ron Huff, whom when I bounce ideas off of, they rebound more concise and fully realized.

Alan Gin, San Francisco's 'Chinese Frank Sinatra'. His wisdom on living the freelance life is always on the mark.

Barney Vinson, casino floor supervisor at Caesars Palace and writer of *Las Vegas: Behind the Tables* and *Casino Secrets*. His personal insights on casino hotel living were invaluable.

Roe Gallo, who has gently pushed me to improve my diet and added to the nutrition section of this book. www.roegallo.com

James 'JimBob' Reinche, who not only invited me to join his fine team of training professionals at MotivationNation, but helped lead the way to my first North American seminar tour. www.motivationnation.com

THE JAMES BOND LIFESTYLE SEMINAR

LIVE THE JAMES BOND LIFESTYLE SEMINAR

CONTENTS

1

A NEW LEADER OF THE PACK

Why James Bond's Lifestyle?

In 1960, Frank Sinatra gathered up Dean Martin, Sammy Davis Jr., Peter Lawford, and Joey Bishop to make a robbery movie in Las Vegas entitled *Ocean's 11*. They acted in the daytime, took a steam in the late afternoon, and performed in the Copa room of the Sands hotel at night. This was the beginning of what would soon be known as "The Rat Pack". For the next five years Sinatra's group would be on the cutting edge of everything that was hip, cool, fun and masculine. In fact, their popularity still continues. Witness the remake of *Ocean's 11*, the new Las Vegas look-a-like show *The Rat Pack Is Back*, and the HBO movie *The Rat Pack*.

But then in 1962 one lone man with a double 0 number came on the scene to be a contender for the number one masculine fantasy icon spot. And that wasn't a Jack Daniel's in his hand, like Frank and the boys had. No, it was a Walther PPK ready to blow away the competition.

The first film, *Dr. No*, attracted attention. The second, *From Russia with Love*, let people know that he was back.

The third, *Goldfinger*, complete with a hat throwing, karate chopping villain, an ejector seat equipped Aston Martin, a hit theme song and a heroine with a name that viewers would only mention in whispers (Pussy Galore), went more gold than the golden girl.

That was 1965. Thirty-seven years and a total of nineteen official films later, James Bond is still the number one male fantasy. His name is spoken when anyone wants to refer to what is masculine and cool. For proof, just keep your ears open and see how many times he is mentioned in other films and in conversations.

The New Bond

In 1967, Sean Connery was in Japan on the six-month shoot of *You Only Live Twice*. In a hotel restroom stall he looked up to see a paparazzo clicking away. That's when he decided that this would be his last Bond film. For a while, it turned out.

Then the big search for Connery's replacement was on. Who would, who could replace him? The answer came in the athletic form of Australian male model George Lazenby. His Bond movie, *On Her Majesty's Secret Service*, would be considered by many purist Bond fans to be the best.

However, when offered a multi-picture deal, what did Lazenby do? He turned the producers down. The producers made a mistake and had gone in to production without having Lazenby sign a long-term contract. They warned him that "You can't make a career out of one Bond film." But the twenty-nine year old Lazenby wouldn't listen. He followed the advice of his agent and turned down future Bond movies. Twelve years later he was interviewed on *Entertainment Tonight* where he looked into the camera and said, "I had my chance and I blew it."

In business and in life there are few things worse than having an opportunity in the palm of your hand and then throwing it away. Even Captain Kangaroo said, "We have to teach our children how to recognize an opportunity."

Here now, in your hands, is an opportunity. An opportunity to live the James Bond Lifestyle.

Your Lifestyle Is Already Good?

Congratulations. That's great. Then you're probably reading this book just out of curiosity. But there is still something very important for you in this book. You'll be able to learn all the techniques that a person needs to turn his life around or upgrade it from where it is. You'll be able to pass this information on to friends and loved ones who may have difficulty making their dreams happen.

I heard an original song once at a concert years ago. I don't remember the singer, as he was not so famous, nor the title. But the first line was, "Love isn't hearts and flowers and walking on the beach. Love is helping someone be what they have to be." I remember being struck by the expression "be what they HAVE to be." I HAD to be a moviemaker. I remember everyone that encouraged me, especially those that took an active part in advancing my career. The greatest thing that you can do for a loved one, is help them be what they have to be. They'll love you for it.

Why Should I Be The One To Teach You?

It's important for you to know who your teacher is, especially since you're spending your time and your money on this book. So if you'll bear with me for just a few pages, I'll share with you my top secret dossier.

Discovering 007

In 1955, three things happened to America that would have an impact on my life. Elvis Presley arrived on the scene bringing with him rock 'n roll, Disneyland opened, and Hugh Hefner released the first issue of *Playboy* magazine. That year also brought the release of Walt Disney's *20,000 Leagues Under The Sea*, starring Kirk Douglas, James Mason and a giant squid.

One night that year, at age 8, I was watching the weekly Disneyland TV show. Walt introduced the night's subject as *The Making of '20,000 Leagues Under the Sea'*. For the next hour I was spell bound watching cameras filming the actors on sets, seeing the story boards of the squid fight, listening to Kirk Douglas talk about working on the film. That night I decided that I wanted to become a moviemaker.

Now you'll have to remember that in those days there were no film schools and nobody talked about directing or producing films outside of Hollywood. So for a small town little boy, this was an unusual idea.

In high school I started making twenty-minute action dramas with my father's 8mm movie camera and enlisting my buddies to act in my 'epics'.

During one summer vacation three of my friends and I went to a drive-in movie to a spy movie called *Dr. No* with an unknown actor, named Sean Connery. I thought the way he judo flipped the bad guys was pretty cool. Then, about an hour into the movie, 'it' happened.

"You've had your six."
Bond in *Dr. No*

'It' came in the form of a scene so unusual that we all sat in the car speechless except for, "Did you see that?"

"Yeah."

Bond is sitting comfortably in a living room chair where he is waiting for the arrival of a henchman who will try to kill him. The killer arrives shooting six bullets into pillows that Bond has stuffed under a sheet. Behind the killer in the dark and still seated, Bond tells him to drop his gun, which he does. As they talk, the killer makes a grab for it and clicks empty at Bond.

With a dead pan face and similar delivery of the next line, except with a hint of sadistic glee, Bond says, "That's a Smith & Wesson and you've had your six." He then shoots the man in the stomach with his silenced Walther PPK. The man spins around and falls to the floor, probably dead. Then Bond, remarkably for any screen hero, puts another silenced bullet into the man's back for good measure. Now this would-be assassin was not a professional killer, like the ones that would come later. No, he was a timid professor. He was scared of Dr. No. He had already failed when trying to kill Bond once before by putting a tarantula in his bed and then came to Dr. No's island when he shouldn't have. I mean this guy could screw up a cup of coffee. And Bond shoots this poor inept man in the back? Bond merely has the woman, who arranged two attempts on his life, arrested, but he coldly kills the weakling.

That was the scene that separated *Dr. No* from all the other spy dramas that came before it. Bond had arrived. But not totally, yet.

"Oh! That was a Bond movie?"

I remember my father telling me about the time he was home alone and felt like going out to a movie. He gave up when he read the entertainment section in our hometown newspaper. He didn't like the sound of what was playing at our local theater. "I wasn't in the mood for a love story, so I didn't go," he said. The love story movie?

From Russia with Love. He groans when he tells that story because after *Goldfinger*, he became a big Bond fan.

I, however, was a big fan from the start. I couldn't quite put my finger on why Bond was so cool. I did know that he could flip guys, so I started flipping guys at our local martial arts studio.

If you were around in 1965, I don't have to tell you what happened with the third Bond movie, *Goldfinger* and the next one *Thunderball*. Bond was giant and the theaters that weren't showing 007 films were showing other spy films. Soon after *The Man from U.N.C.L.E.* became a big hit spy series on the tube.

So now, what follows is a true story that would set me off on a search for the Bond mystic and the Bond lifestyle more than any of the movies, the Fleming novels, or the Karate classes. Pay attention to this.

Her Husband a Secret Agent?

During 1966, the year of *Thunderball*, I was going to college and working at a gas station part time. One day an attractive woman in her thirties pulled up for some gas. When she handed me her credit card I noticed it had a man's name on it: John Dangerfield. Not knowing of Rodney Dangerfield at the time, and being Bond crazy, I separated the man's last name in my mind and said to the woman with an excited comical tone of voice, "Dangerfield? Is your husband a secret agent?"

Now, I was expecting a chuckle or a joke back. But instead, she looked at me, then hung her head down, shook it slowly from side to side, and gave a sad and disappointed, "No … no."

Her seriousness caught me off guard and I didn't know how to respond so I just processed her purchase without further word.

I remember thinking at the time, that if someone asked my girlfriend or future wife if I was a secret agent, any comical answer would be okay, like: "In his dreams" or "Well, he's trying" or "Maybe he thinks he is." Anything would be acceptable, but not a disappointed shake of the head and a "No … no."

That's when I decided that I should do something about being like James Bond. Yes, taking karate was a good step, so was studying filmmaking. But I knew that was not enough. Not nearly. I had to do something else. I didn't know what. But from that time on, I watched Bond on the screen with more than just enjoyment. I watched him for the answers. Answers to questions like, Why is he cool? Why do both men and women like him? How can I have his excitement without the danger of actually going on a mission? Why does he always seem to win at gambling? Where does his self-confidence come from?

I didn't know it at the time, but the real question that was buried away in my subconscious was "Who pays for all those resort hotels?"

I didn't pursue these questions whole heartedly for years. They floated in and out of my mind with the arrival of each new Bond movie and with each re-viewing of the old movies.

Once I watched a double bill of *Thunderball* and *You Only Live Twice*, twice through, entering the theater at noon and leaving at 8 PM. I guess I survived on popcorn and soda that day.

The Secret of Bond Hidden in Your Mind

At the age of 25 I raised enough money to write, produce and direct my first feature in 35mm Techniscope, called *Drawn Swords*. It was a period film about three

Samurai going to England and fighting knights because they weren't allowed to enter a sword fighting tournament.

My movie has the dubious distinction of being the only black and white Techniscope movie ever made or ever will be, given the fact that this process was made strictly for color. Also, this wide screen process, which photographed half frame 35mm film, is no longer used. That choice of filming in black and white was the blunder, which put me into debt and almost kept me from pursuing my life's dream – making more feature films.

Out of work and with all my monthly funds going to pay the loans on my worthless (because of it's being shot in black and white) film, I found myself at the bookstore browsing instead of going to the movies. I remember so clearly seeing that yellow book lying face up on the bottom shelf near my feet. Its name? *The Million Dollar Secret Hidden in Your Mind*, by Anthony Norvell.

With a title like that, and with my need for cash so great, I was immediately interested. By imitating Akira Kurosawa's black and white filmmaking style, I had dug myself into a hole. I needed to get out; I picked up the book. After thumbing through it, I bought it and took that first step into that 'larger world' that Obi-Wan Kanobi talks about.

"I mean, he reads EVERYTHING."
Cliff Robertson talking about Robert Redford
in *Three Days of the Condor*

The book is about taking the limitations off of your thinking in all areas of your life; it was the mind-altering experience that it claimed to be. From there I began buying any book that even hinted at the possibility of a successful lifestyle. Which meant, like 'The Condor', who was an innocent swept up into an adventure of survival, I read everything. My apartment became a 'fortress of solitude' from where I would study every self-help book that I could find. Books on the subconscious mind, money, memory and success.

Then I really got lucky when I drove down from San Francisco to Los Angeles on my thirtieth birthday. Searching the entertainment section of the LA Times at my sister's apartment, I saw an ad that said Anthony Norvel of the *Million Dollar Secret* was giving classes at the Wilshire Ebell theater in the heart of the 'Miracle Mile'. It was ten minutes before the eleven AM class started. It would take me twenty minutes to drive there, but as much as I hate showing up late for something, I told my sister I'd be back for an afternoon movie and vaulted out the door.

I arrived to see Norvel, then in his seventies and just back from retirement from his home on Mt. Olympus in Greece, talking on stage with the lighting giving him a halo effect. His words of empowerment, success, and unlimited thinking went straight into me, like a positive golden arrow. I signed up for four two hour classes a week and spent the next three months studying the laws of success with the master who had started out in the forties in Hollywood being the advisor to the stars. And what great stories he had.

When summer ended, I returned to San Francisco determined to raise the $200,000 financing for my next movie. It came in six weeks.

A year after that, I happened to turn my car radio knob to search for something other than music (something I never did), and ended up hearing a success show. It was taught by a prosperity teacher named Marc Reymont and he was the next level above what I had learned with Norvel. For three years I took lessons from him until he passed away leaving no book to record his unique methods. These methods I altered to fit my way of approaching life's challenges and use to this day.

Besides the self help books, I read biographies on successful people, ranging from actors I admired to Ray Kroc, the 'golden arches' man himself who certainly had to overcome greater challenges than I had to get his McDonald's hamburger business off the ground. And here I thought I was the only one having business problems, the only one who was having a tough time making his dream come true. No, there were others out there and by reading their books, I now had 'friends in high places', if you will.

While all of this was happening there was Bond. Bond always lurking in the back of my mind as the ultimate expression of a successful lifestyle. I was disappointed that Sean Connery and George Lazenby were gone and with them (for the next two Bond films) so would go the wide screen, the budget and the seriousness. Oh sure, I liked Roger Moore. I had since he started appearing on the *Maverick* TV show, but he wasn't the same as Connery or Lazenby with their dark suave athletic Bond portrayals.

Yet, *The Man with the Golden Gun* got me back into the spirit of Bond or perhaps it was the villain. Christopher Lee played Scaramanga, the assassin who kills for a million dollars with one shot from his gold gun. He does this after making love to psych himself up for the hit. Now there's a guy with some style, except for the killing part.

It's 007 Who Takes Me To A New Level

New Bond films came and went. I got a few more feature films produced, and then home video came on the market. I think that's what started to solidify the idea of really making an effort to live the life that 007 was leading. Seeing Bond on my living room TV, commercial free, any time I wanted was great. Just like *The Wizard of Oz* only became popular when it was televised and viewed in people's homes, Bond became more personal when I viewed him alone.

As the Bond movies increased in number, my lifestyle improved, only slowly. But it did move up and that thought sustained me as I maintained a freelance money-earning situation.

Being hired to direct a travel video in Phuket, Thailand where *The Man with the Golden Gun* was filmed put it all together for me. Because of a glitch in travel arrangements my crew went ahead of me and I flew to Hong Kong by myself. Arranging my connection to Bangkok and then Phuket, I was informed there was a special flight leaving at seven AM and I could take that if I wanted. I took it.

When I boarded the Cathy Pacific 747 airliner, six Thai flight attendants greeted me. It turned out I was the only passenger on the entire plane and with a first class ticket arranged by the producer. "Take any seat you want," one of the attendants said while the others disappeared to their stations in the empty plane. I chose a seat in the back of first class.

Even with only one passenger aboard, regulations required the reading and demonstration of the safety regulations, which were not, at that time, on video. The attractive attendant who did the demonstrating walked up to where I was sitting, stood right in front of me and said with a smile, "For your eyes only." Finally, I was Bond.

That's right. It's a true story. It actually happened. This pretty woman standing three feet in front of me says, *For Your Eyes Only*, the title of the Bond movie that was just out, as well as the song by Sheena Easton. Was I dreaming?

After finishing her demonstration she took my breakfast

order, gave me an American newspaper and headed off towards the galley. I wasn't much interested in reading the paper, but when I unfolded it, I saw that the front page had the listings of who won the Academy Awards the night before. I had missed the show and here were the results handed to me as I headed off for *Golden Gun* territory.

After I finished eating the specially prepared omelet, the British co-pilot came out of the cockpit and introduced himself. He was curious why I happened to be aboard a flight that usually had no passengers and was mainly for cargo (even though it had a complete flight crew because of union regulations). After I explained he invited me to sit in the cockpit behind the pilot for the last part of the flight.

Later I read in *Charlton Heston's Diary* that he was invited into the cockpit a few years earlier, but "the regulations had tightened, because of hijackings and not even celebrities were allowed in the cockpit anymore." Well, I don't know about celebrities, but Paul Kyriazi, a la James Bond, was invited, not only into the cockpit, but to remain there for the landing.

Later, sitting in the Bangkok airport restaurant waiting for my flight to Phuket, I thought over my *For Your Eyes Only* flight and about directing the upcoming video in the beautiful "Bond location" resort island. I knew I wanted this to continue. I knew, however, it would take more jobs, more success, more money, and above all, a plan.

When I returned to America, I viewed my copy of *The Man with the Golden Gun* again. Then I viewed my favorite Bond films, *Dr. No*, *From Russia with Love*, *On Her Majesty's Secret Service* and *You Only Live Twice*. It was during that week that I started to jot down a few notes. I knew that I didn't want to be Bond, but that I wanted to live like him. Does this mean that I wanted adventure and danger? No, I wasn't interested in sky diving, mountain climbing nor going on mercenary missions in some jungle. What was I looking for? Why was Bond a different hero than say, Rambo, Dirty Harry or Rocky?

Then it finally clicked. Before Bond goes on a mission he's usually at a resort hotel, casino or lying in a boat with Sylvia Trench with a bottle of Dom Pérignon hanging from a string into the river. Before Rambo goes on a mission he's in prison or on some mountain top temple fighting for his daily bowl of rice. Dirty Harry lives in a dark cheap apartment and Rocky in a cheaper one. Ah, ha! That's it! Bond is not only a man of action, as all heroes are, he is also a man of leisure. Yes, leisure. I liked the sound of that. Yes, that suits my style. I always liked to work hard (on movies and writing anyway) and play hard (in Las Vegas, concerts, movies, amusement parks and resorts).

From that time on, everything I learned about a successful lifestyle I framed in terms of James Bond. Every category of lifestyle from budgeting my money, to travel, to my apartment, to business, would have James Bond as the foundation. Was using a fictional character as a role model juvenile and unproductive? No, I didn't think so. But what about using real men as role models?

What about Frank Sinatra whom I admired? Wasn't he the closest thing to Bond with his tuxedo? Wasn't he living a very productive glamorous lifestyle? Sure he was.

Sinatra was filming the western *Sergeants 3* in the Arizona desert. On one action scene he paid off his stunt double to NOT do a stunt so that he, himself could be seen on camera dragging under a runaway buckboard. He actually did that stunt among others. After that, at night, he and his pal Dean Martin helicoptered into Las Vegas to do two shows at the Sands Hotel. He did this day and night for the length of the filming, using weekends to record in Los Angeles. Now that's what I call being productive.

Still, he always played. Played with his buddies at resorts and nightclubs around the world, while still turning out an incredible body of work in films, concerts and records.

But alas, Frank Sinatra was human and given to human errors and imperfections. No, it would have to be Bond for me, fictional or not.

I End Up Doing A Bond Movie

Was it a dream? No, it was real.

There I was on the set of *View To A Kill*, not directing alas, but acting. A friend who was working as an extra invited me to be in the City Hall fire scene, where Bond climbs down the ladder carrying the girl. There is a shot of the firemen taking a man on stretcher out the front door and down the steps of the building. It is a fairly long running shot and I am easily visible wearing a white zipper jacket. (The guy with the blond hair.) It wasn't a big part; in fact, it wasn't a part at all. I was just an extra, but I really got into the feeling of the scene. See the look of concern on my face?

I took this as a good omen of things to come and it was. A few years later, I was hired to be the voice of James Bond in a Carlsberg Beer TV commercial that was also advertising the new Bond movie. And I was doing it in *You Only Live Twice* land. That's right, Japan. I had only one word to say, "Carlsberg." Still, for that recording session, I was Bond.

The Bond Lifestyle Becomes the Written Word

Being freelance and working on many projects and coming into contact with many new people, the subject of freelance success often comes up in conversation. It's then, and only then that I'm asked (which is often), "How are you able to do all these projects, go to all these places, live in two countries (USA and Japan) and manage to do it as a freelance with no company or sponsor behind you on a permanent basis?"

I've spent a lot of time with so many people explaining my 007 lifestyle techniques, but I often forget to tell them an important aspect; so I decided to get it all down on tape. Thus, my audio book was born. But even the three-hour seminars that I was invited to weren't long enough to include all of what I thought was important for quickly upgrading ones' lifestyle. Thus this book.

This Is For A Serious Minded Person Who Takes Action

That's right! This book is for you. You paid the price. Make one dream come true. *You Only Live Twice*.

Well, I'm not so much of a metaphysician to know if we live twice or not. One thing I do know is that you're on the planet right now. So why should James Bond have all the fun, all the resorts, all the cash and all the adventure? It's time to claim yourself a piece of it. You know, we go to Bond movies and we cheer for him. "Come on, 007. Forget the pain. Don't mind the danger. Keep going. Don't give up." But when we come out of the theater we forget about rooting for ourselves. We think, "I'd like to get my University degree, but it's too much trouble. I'd like to ask that girl out on a date, but she'll probably turn me down and if she says yes, it'll be too expensive. I'd like to start my own business, but it's too risky. I'd like to get into shape, but it's too hard giving up junk food." Now it's time to get your 'butt' out of the way. Time to take action. Time to run while others walk, to act while others just talk. Time to look at this world and want it all, and then strike, like *Thunderball*.

Because I can't motivate you and you can't motivate me, this is about the only motivation that you'll get from this book. It's the power that is in you that you must call upon to motivate yourself. Remember that old Leo Sayer song, *You Make Me Feel Like Dancing*? Well, you don't make me feel like dancing. I make me feel like dancing. It's me, reacting to you that make me feel like dancing. Another person may look at you and feel like running or laughing, or whatever.

So the rest of this book is filled with techniques, not motivation. I do promise you with my hand over my heart, that if you follow these techniques, in the first week you'll see improvement in your life; after the first month, a different outlook and after six months, you will see the Bond in you appear. This course won't make you Bond, but it will make you, you. A healthy you that is living the James Bond lifestyle.

Secrets of the Universe

Playing Lex Luther in *Superman*, Gene Hackman says, "Why is it that some people read *Moby Dick* and come away thinking it a mere adventure story? While others read the ingredients on the back of a chewing gum wrapper and unlock secrets of the universe?"

The same could hold true for you and this book.

2

YOUR BASE OF OPERATIONS

The first thing that you'll need to start off your mission is a base of operations, and you're probably sitting in it right now. Look around your place for a moment. Is it clean, organized, comfortable? Are you ready to entertain if your doorbell should ring?

In the movie *Dr. No* we get a rare look at Bond's apartment. Pull out your copy of the film and take a look at it. (It's exactly fifteen minutes into the movie.) Note there is no clutter. It's clean and organized. When Bond comes home and finds that Miss Trench has let herself in and is waiting for him, he doesn't have to give out with the trite excuse, "Forgive the mess." No, he can pursue a more productive and entertaining course of conversation.

Observe Bond's office. The only time we see it is in *On Her Majesty's Secret Service* (*OHMSS*). Not a bit of clutter or disorganization to be seen. Look at his bulletin board on the wall. Not the usual mess of notes, but well organized papers connected by a red tape line. Take a look at the table under it. It has only a few books and papers on it.The table is ready for any work that may come up. His desk also has lots of open space for him to do his work. Even space enough for him to put a suitcase to pack when he decides to quit the secret service.

Note: I find it ironic that Lazenby quit the series just like Bond decided to quit his job. Except fortunately for Bond, Miss Moneypenny submitted a two-week leave request, instead of a resignation request. Too bad George didn't have an interested friend to sidetrack his resignation.

Okay. Let's get to it. Everything in the James Bond lifestyle starts in your mind. Your thoughts are your mental words. "In the beginning was the word," if you will. From there your actions radiate from your body and interact with the world around you. Clear organized thinking begets a clear organized environment. We'll work on the all-important mental techniques later. For now, organizing your immediate environment is a comparatively easy (but essential) first action step. The good news is that you don't have to start with your entire apartment.

Your Mission Control Center

Find a convenient place in your apartment where you can have about a two by three-foot space on a table, desk, or kitchen counter, to set up your mission control center. This could preferably be a space next to your personal computer. Clean this space of any articles, dirt and dust. This space will now forever remain clean and dust free, no matter what shape your apartment is in during various times of the month. This space stays clean, period. This space represents your mind in the physical world. Here will go your most important tools to live an organized life and to plan all your missions, trips education, dreams and goals. As far as the physical world goes, for you, everything starts here.

Q Branch's Most Important Tools

Now what could those be? A transmitter that fits conveniently in the heel of your shoe so that you can be tracked by your team members? Exploding pens that will help you escape your captors? A Walther PPK with "the impact of a brick going through a plate glass window?" Not hardly. The two most important tools for anyone on a mission are the calendar and the calculator.

The calendar is used to set the date of your mission, be it a trip, the beginning of a new course of study, the date you plan to move to a new apartment or to purchase a new car. The calculator is used to make up the budget requirements for that particular mission.

Let's take each of these tools separately. Examining the power of each. And please don't skim over this part just because these tools don't sound as exciting to you as a car ejector seat. Believe me, they have much more power than that. Because the tools of time and money (energy) are all powerful. Time and energy can build mountains or wear them down. In fact, when you start to think about it, you'll realize that all you have on this planet is time and energy (money being the symbol of energy).

You Have All The Time In The World

That was the song sung by Louie Armstrong in *OHMSS* and also the line repeated in the film by Bond. (And yes, for you film historians, it was a line from *The Time Machine*.) But my favorite movie quote about time is in

Gone With the Wind. "Do not squander time. That is the stuff life is made of."

There are dozens of books on time management at the bookstore and as many systems, both electronic and notebook, that will help organize your time. Before you decide which system to use, let's start with the basics. A simple invention known as the calendar.

Run out to the stationary store and get a desk top style calendar. The one with the open squares for each day. (No lines inside the squares.) It will have one page per month on a hard cardboard backing. Not too big, not too small. The ones covered with a flip over plastic sheet will protect your writing and give a nice clean feel to it. The reason that you need the hard cardboard backing is so that you can pick it up anytime, sit down on your sofa with it on your lap and plan with it. And for this reason you will need a pen that is to your liking, always clipped to your calendar, so you don't have to go searching for something to write with when you get a brainstorm. And, for that matter, you should have a few spare pens on your "mission control center" space, as well.

What? You already have a calendar hanging on your wall with a photo of Mt. Shasta? Great! Keep it there and enjoy it, but go out and get your "Q Branch" calendar that will be a special and powerful symbol for your new lifestyle. You've already got a palm pilot? That's great, too. Some people love them; others stop using them after a few months and go back to the address book type. Which ever you use, go out and get the calendar as well.

When you look at your calendar, realize that each of those squares represents a day of your time, your life. When you go to work, you are selling one of those squares to your company for that day's pay. Likewise when a "friend" pushes you to accompany him to an event that you are not interested in, and in fact might be counter-productive to your life, you are giving him one or more squares of your life. Hopefully, this idea will get you to appreciate your days and look at them in a new and valuable light.

Setting the Activation Date

Definite plans get definite results. What do indefinite plans get you? Did you answer "indefinite results"? If you did, you're wrong. Indefinite plans get you ... NO results ... definitely. That's why there has to be an activation date put on your mission plan. That's why we start with the calendar. However, setting a date is scary.

Most people will come up with any excuse to not set a date. I've seen this in the movie business. Committing to a start date is hard for producers, because such large amounts of money are at stake. Even a simple five day trip can have the same paralyzing effect on a guy if he is on a limited budget, or if he's cheap, or a natural procrastinator, or not sure if the trip is what he wants to do, or if the girl he's taking is worth taking, or ... on and on.

But a date must be set for a plan to have power. For it to ever be acted upon. Set the date once you've decided your mission, be it a large or small mission. Be it next week, next month, or next year. And set the actual day date, as in June 4th, not sometime in June. This is a powerful step toward your mission. Simple, but powerful. So simple in fact (as many of the upcoming techniques are), that people often give the standard lip service reply of "Yeah, yeah, I know that," but never get a calendar, let alone set a date to take action on their dreams. They'll say, "Maybe I'll go to Las Vegas in the summer. But I might go to New Orleans, or maybe I'll go after the summer. Or perhaps I'll visit New York. Maybe

I'll just wait and see."This guy will most likely stay home and watch reruns of *Gilligan's Island*.

"I'm going to San Francisco on July 3rd. I will stay for five nights.The budget will be $1,700. I will stay at the Fisherman's Wharf Sheraton Inn. I will take tours in the day time and see some shows at night." You know that this guy is going, for sure.

Q's Simplest, Yet Powerful Gadget

"Make sure you bring it back from the field, 007."
"Oh, you'd be surprised how hard it is out there in the field."
Bond and Q in *Goldfinger*

You won't take this gadget out into the field. This gadget you'll keep at your mission control center, always. Yes, I've already mentioned it. The simple calculator. To calculate the financial energy needed to accomplish your missions. Get a desk size, eight-inch type so you can easily see and hit the buttons, programming your mind that money is handled easily by you. (More on programming the mind later.)

You can get a wallet size calculator to take out in the field with you to do continuing budget status checks, in case you're playing it close to your cash and credit limits on an important mission. But get the large size for your mission control center.

Completing Your Mission Control Center

Besides your calendar and calculator, you will put your wallet, keys, glasses, money clip and address book there when they're not in your pockets. From now on, if they aren't there you'd better start looking for them, because they're lost. Having these items there will stop those time wasting searches for the articles you need everyday in the field. This is your power base, your planning space and your thinking base. The books that you are reading in order to move your life forward will also go here.

Once again, no matter what the order and cleanliness of your apartment, this space stays clean and organized. It will only take a minute to dust and arrange, so there can't be any excuses for it not being as it should.

From this base, you will extend your control and order to your apartment, then out to your car, then to your job space, then to your town or city. Meaning the places you frequent for shopping, socializing, car maintenance, haircuts and so on. Next comes control of places that you take short trips to. This means knowing the hotels you like to stay in and the services you need in that area. Next comes understanding the world, as in places you want to visit someday and what hotels you'll start off at. Next ... well, if *The World Is Not Enough* (Bond's family motto on his coat of arms) then you'll be ready to examine psychological, philosophical and metaphysical ideas.

Your base of operations and control center are the cornerstones of your missions and overall advancement. Start working on them first.

Bond Symbols For Change

To really make a long lasting commitment to living a Bondlike lifestyle, you'll have to have a few symbolic gadgets around to remind you of that commitment on a daily basis, so as not to backslide into your old habits. These gadgets you'll get, of course, from Q. These include, but are not limited to:

1. **A new money clip**. If you've never used a money

clip you'll find this to be an energizing experience. Having cash, not only in your wallet, but in your front pocket exposed, so to speak, without being hidden by leather, makes one feel like he's got a powerful backup in case he forgets or loses his wallet someplace. So go to a department or jewelry store, they have them for as little as $10, and pick out one that suits you. They have them in all types with all sorts of symbols on them or just plain. Mine has a secret blade in it. I can't tell you how many times I've used it for cutting string and opening envelopes. Once you purchase it, neatly fold some cash in half and put it in the clip and into your front pocket. Later, in the money section of this course, there will be further ideas on this Bond prosperity symbol. And to repeat, this will go on your mission control space when not in your pocket.

2. **A new wallet.** This, of course will hold your big bills and credit cards. This is the symbol of the new attitude that you will soon have about cash. Every time you pull it out of your pocket you will think, "Ah yes, my new wallet. I'm supposed to be thinking differently about money. And I will. I am."

3. **A new watch.** Don't worry, it doesn't have to be an Omega like Bond now uses. Or the Rolex he used in *Goldfinger*. In fact, you should be holding your finances for other areas in your life right now. Just get a new watch so that every time you look at it, you'll be reminded that you've made a commitment to upgrade your life and to follow the guidelines that you've set to take action on your goals.

Later, say in six months, once you've proven to yourself that you are living the Bond lifestyle on a permanent basis, you can get something more expensive, as long as you buy it because you like it and it empowers you, not because you want to impress others with it. When I did buy a watch that was many times more expensive than I was used to, it actually did empower me more than I thought it might. But be forewarned, wearing an expensive watch means upgrading your thinking, talking and acting. Plus you would look ridiculous asking anyone to borrow a few bucks till payday while wearing an expensive watch. So before you get that watch, be sure the finances in your wallet and money clip can handle the new energy level that you've supposedly risen to.

So put a new watch on your list of gadgets to get from Q branch and get it soon. And never miss a chance when checking the time to say to yourself, "That's right, this new watch is telling me that I've changed. That my thoughts, words and actions are now on a higher level than before and they're more energized than before. I will never forget this commitment."

4. **A new attaché case**. Yeah, have it look like the one in *From Russia with Love*. Put it near or on your mission control space. You don't have to take it out of the house with you, if that's not your habit. But this is a powerful symbol and a handy thing to keep important and pending papers in. You may need to use it out in the field on occasion, so it will be there waiting for you. You'll want to keep it dusted and clean. If you want, you can go out and buy a couple of gold coins to put in it, just for fun and more prosperity programming. I wouldn't recommend the fifty gold sovereigns just now, nor the tear-gas, sniper's rifle or throwing dagger.

5. **A James Bond movie title song anthology on CD**. Just the thing to play in the morning to remind you that things are different now. To energize you towards the day's action.

I like Tom Jones singing *Thunderball*. Knowing that poor Tom fainted in the recording booth holding that last powerful note and giving his all, really inspires me to give it my all, too. *Goldfinger* is great when you want to get in the prosperous mood and have "the Midas touch." *Diamonds Are Forever* gets your mind and feelings (subconscious energy) turned on for unlimited prosperity as well. Keep the CD in your player and use it when you need a boost: when you need Tom, Shirley, or Sheena to encourage you on your chosen path to your destiny.

6. **A couple of your favorite Bond videos to watch in part or totally when you need encouragement**. There's nothing like seeing Bond walking through luxury resorts to make you say, "Yeah, that's right. I'm going there, too. And soon."

7. **Subscribe to a few new magazines**. One concerned with health and fitness. (Bond is always healthy. Beat up sometimes, but healthy.) One concerning money. One concerning an activity that you want to start getting more involved in, such as travel, education, aviation or any new hobby. Of course, you can get this information via internet magazines and newsletters, and that's great. But to receive them in the mail is like getting a reminder from outside that tells you to continue your positive action. Put these magazines on a visible space, such as on your coffee table or kitchen counter for you to see often during the course of your day.

8. **Subscribe to free internet newsletters from success sites on the net**. You can find them by searching things like 'success', 'self-help', 'empowerment' and so on. There's a lot of negative and limiting programming hitting

us everyday. To counterbalance this we need as much positive re-enforcement coming to us from as many different angles as possible.

9. **A personal computer**, if you don't have one. At least set up an email address that you can access. Email is all-important now for communication, both business and social, not to mention the internet for fast information on all of your goals. No need to buy travel books for your destination these days. Just search the name of the place you want to go and you have more information on it than an encyclopedia could hold. This is the one expensive item on this list, but a computer will be necessary for you in the future. It doesn't have to be new. It doesn't have to have all the fancy programs. As long as it has email and internet capabilities, it will enter you into a new world of communication, planning and education.

These Bond Lifestyle Symbols Are Important

Don't think of this step as too easy that you fail to do it. Don't let the idea that you have to shell out a few gold sovereigns stop you from it, either. This is a very powerful step to have your environment in control. You want to have your space constantly visually and aurally programming you to continue on towards success.

Later we'll talk about the needed thinking that must occur for your new lifestyle to solidify. But for now, put your base of operations, mission control space and your Q Branch tools together. It's easy and will be needed to back you up when you start taking action and planning your missions.

The upcoming techniques will be more difficult to put into action so lay the ground work with these easy, yet powerful ones first.

3

BOND AND HIS CASH

In high school I can remember my buddies and I talking about the briefcase that Bond used in *From Russia with Love*. We talked about how cool it was that it was rigged with exploding gas if opened improperly. How it came equipped with a sniper's rifle, throwing dagger and a device to see if the phone was bugged.

However, I remember after I got out of college and talked with a friend about that movie. The conversation went as follows:

"*From Russia with Love* is one of my favorite Bond films," I said.

"Yeah, it was great."

"Do you remember what was in his attaché case?"

"Yeah, fifty gold sovereigns," he answered abruptly and emphatically. He answered with only that. The reason being once you get out of college money becomes of great importance, if not before that.

Later on in this course I will give you the 21 rules for living the James Bond lifestyle. But I'll give you two of them right now.

Rule #1- Never run out of cash.

If we skip down to the last rule it reads:

Rule #21- Never run out of cash.

No, that's not a printing error. That's exactly what it is. Now, if you concentrate on rule #1 and rule #21, the other 19 rules kind of take care of themselves. This is no joke. Yes, a loving relationship is more important than money. I agree, but with money being the reported cause of eighty percent of American divorces, I guess the Beatles' song, *Money Can't Buy Me Love*, was written on a false assumption. Money can buy you love. In fact, twenty years later George Harrison finally got it right with his song, *I've Got My Mind Set On You*. In that song, talking about a newly developing love relationship, he says that "it's going to take a whole lot of spending money to do it right."

The True Meaning of Success

You've heard many definitions of success. Most of them are meaningful. Some difficult to imagine or do. But here is the best definition of success that I've heard of. This one cuts right to the core and is easy to understand and points clearly to the road that you should take and the mental satisfaction that you should have. The definition is this: Success is enjoying your time.

Think about what this means to you. To me it means doing more of the things that you want to do and less of the things that you don't want to do. Money is one of the biggest tools that will help you accomplish just that.

"Say Q, what is money, anyway?"
"Oh, grow up 007."

What is money? Sounds like a simple question doesn't it? Can you answer it? It takes a little thought to come up with a descriptive, yet concise, answer.

Simply put, money is a symbol of energy. Before the advent of money, the barter system was used. People traded farm goods, products and services. They paid their debts with cows, shoes and eggs. Of course, that couldn't continue for too long, otherwise we'd have to give six eggs to a taxi driver for a ride. And what if the fare comes to five and a half eggs? The soldiers of Rome were paid with salt. Hence the expression, "He's not worth his salt." The Roman word for salt was 'Salarium' and this is where we get the word 'salary'.

Next came precious metals and then paper symbolizing these precious metals to make exchanges of goods and services easier. Right, we learned that in second grade. But it's good to start from this point so that we can get to the next one, which is: If money is the symbol of energy, is this energy positive or negative? Want to take a guess?

Money's energy is neither positive nor negative. Money is the symbol of neutral energy. It just depends on how you use it. It's like dirt. You can use dirt to grow a tree and eat the apples from it. Or you can put that dirt in your orange juice, drink it and get sick from it. In both cases the dirt was just being the dirt. Your action made it positive or negative.

The main thing to remember here is that the more energy you have, the more positive energy you can manifest. Or the more negativity you can create. Put another way: with a little money you can have a little good influence or a little bad influence. But with a lot of money you can do a lot of good things or a lot of bad things. So gathering and controlling this energy and ultimately using it for something positive is what we have to consider in our lives.

Money is a living energy. An energy that we must establish a constructive relationship with. A relationship where we don't scare it away, but attract it. Where we can use it, instead of it using us. We will address this delicate relationship here in this all-important chapter.

Rich vs. Prosperous

Bond is rich. Bond is prosperous. What's the difference? A big one, I'd say. Rich is a lot of money in the bank, period. And that's good. Prosperous is good money circulation in your life. Where the cash comes in to meet your chosen lifestyle, with some left over to save for future needs. But not saved for a 'rainy day'. Save for a rainy day, attract a rainy day. Save for an upcoming positive event or item.

Prosperity also includes health, the right work, good friends, a comfortable place to live, hope for a greater future and any other things that adds … 'good livingness' to your time on the planet. Rich is great and not something to be shunned. But without the attributes of prosperity, especially health, rich alone doesn't get it done. Not by half.

This is not to say that we use this as an excuse to not get rich. Be careful of that mind trap. This just means to include all the positive things in your life, when you decide to go for more money and a higher standard of living. So from now on we will use the word prosperity which also includes the idea of being rich.

Programming the Mind for Prosperity

We'll go into the details of the mind in an upcoming chapter, but for now be assured that your mind, particularly your subconscious mind, is recording every thought, word, image and feeling that you experience. Then it goes about attracting those energies into your real experience. It does this by subconsciously guiding you into situations, choices and groups of people that will help make these mind recordings become real. Thus, your attitudes, feelings and images of money are impressed on your mind and you'll attract prosperity or lack of it. You'll often hear from wealthy people that, "Wealth is a state of mind." The unenlightened might answer, "Yeah, and it's also a state of your bank account." They'd be right also, to a point. Now, let's examine this all-important point that they are missing.

Bond's Money Attitude

Bond always has cash. He always tips. He wears nice clothes. Yet, he never talks about money. I guess he doesn't have to because he has it. Yet, he's a government service man. A mercenary of sorts, true, but there is a limit to his salary being in government service. Yet, he never has any money worries on his mind. How does he go to all those nice resorts when he's off duty and not on his job per diem? He has to account for those gold sovereigns; they are not his to spend.

My guess is that wherever he gets his dough, he's got his mind together when it comes to money. He certainly has enough of it for his lifestyle because in *OHMSS* he easily turned down Draco's million-dollar offer to marry his daughter. "But I don't need a million dollars," he said.

Let's Begin Our Programming For Prosperity

Appreciate what you have now. That's the very first step to take. For example, someone might say, "I'd like to start a business, but I don't have an office, or a computer, or a cell phone, or business cards. I guess I can't go into business."

The key here is start with what you do have. Repeat: Start with what you do have. Look around. You've got a spare table, a calculator, a calendar, a phone, pens, paper, oh yes, your apartment itself. Set up that table, put these items on it and start from there. Simple? Yes, very. Still, few people do it. It's easier to use the lack of materials and capital as an excuse to not do something. For the third time: Start with what you do have. Have constant appreciation for it. From that point, you will be guided to take right action to get the other things you need to start achieving your mission.

Bond Is Trapped With Nothing To Use For Escape

In *OHMSS*, Bond is trapped in the wheel room of a ski lift. His only avenue of escape is the narrow opening where the cable exits the room. But between it and him is a wide space with a long drop. If he could only grab the freezing cable, hang from it and work his way up to the opening. What to do? The villain's henchmen put him in there with no gloves, tools, nothing.

Does Bond moan, "I can't do it. I don't have gloves, or a rope, or a blow torch"? No. He improvises, adapts and overcomes. He uses what he has. What does he have? Pockets. That's right. Remember? He tears out his pocket linings and uses them for gloves and climbs out. Later, he manages to get to some skis and escape down the mountain. Bond used what he had and overcame his obstacles to carry out his mission. So can we.

Two Sources Of Cash On Your Body

To repeat, go to Q Branch and get issued a money clip. (If you haven't already.) There's a big psychological edge to carrying a money clip, as well as convenience.

First of all, you'll have cash in two places. Your wallet and your front pocket. If you lose one you'll still have the other. A pickpocket or mugger will always go for your wallet. Therefore, you'll have cash in your money clip to get you were you have to go and do what you have to do that day.

Put large bills in your wallet. Like a couple of hundreds and fifties to have on hand for restaurants that might not take credit cards or when their card processor is on the blink. Twenties and smaller denominations go in your money clip. The real convenience of this is that you'll be able to pay for most things with the cash in your clip, without having to reach for your wallet. Anytime you pull out your wallet you risk losing something and it's troublesome to replace contents like driver's license and credit cards, not to mention being marked for set up by a pickpocket. In addition, a money clip in your front pocket is easier to get to than your wallet when your hands are full.

A mind-programming step to use with your money clip is always have the outside bill be a hundred. When you pay for things just flip past it and go to the second bill. (If you're not used to paying by money clip you can practice in your home.) Having a large bill on the outside of your clip is not meant to impress others, in fact you'll have to make sure the wrong type of people don't see it. The hundred-dollar bill on the outside is to program you for larger sums of money. Also you don't feel worried about spending the money in your clip if you know that there's a hundred in it backing you up (as well as those in your wallet).

To double this programming, put another hundred in

the very inside of your half folded bills. You'll always know that it's there even when you don't see it. And when you've spent your last small bill, if you haven't had the chance to replenish your clip, you'll end up with the hundred-dollar bill on the inside as well on the outside. Now that's prosperity programming.

You'll find out all kinds of conveniences when you start using your clip. You can buy different types of clips depending of the thickness of the cash you carry. But the one that you often carry should have some special meaning for you.

Note: The only time we see Bond's money clip is just a flash when Donald Grant takes it from the unconcious Bond lying on the floor of the train in *From Russia With Love*.

The Color of Money

The Color of Money is the sequel to *The Hustler*. In that film Paul Newman kept his money folded in his shirt pocket without a money clip. When he paid off a bet he would put it on the pool table folded and standing up "pup tent" style. This made it easy to see and easy to pick up by the person he was paying. In fact, this is how they do it at casino gaming tables, as no money is passed from hand to hand. It is first placed on the table for all to see, including the TV cameras, thereby eliminating mistakes of denomination.

You might try using that style when there is a counter to put the money on. This way the clerk you are paying sees it, but can pick it up when he is finished with his ringing up the tab or bagging your groceries. Also with that hard crease in the folded money it's easy to identify in the cash drawer should the clerk make a mistake as to the denomination.

I really like setting the bills down like that. It's sort of a ritual that prepares the money for changing hands. It gives the feeling of a final respect for that particular cash before being cast on the water and then circulating back.

Give it a try. If it suits you, continue using it.

WARNING: If you are in grade school or high school, don't carry large amounts of money. Word goes out fast to everyone in school and you'll soon be marked for carrying a lot of cash in a place where low vibrational students will do an Oddjob on you just to get some vintage Pokemon cards, let alone a wad of cash.

Likewise, for you graduated guys, be careful not to let your 'friends' turn you into a human cash dispenser for quick loans whenever they need it. Twice is enough for dubious friends, and only if they've paid you back when they said they would. After that, be sure to leave your big cash at home when you go to meet that particular friend.

And of course, never pull out your money clip when 'unfriendlies' are lurking about in an unfamiliar area. Reach into your pocket and slip the needed bills out of your clip unseen to make your purchase.

Old Blue Eyes And His Pointed Gold Money Clip

Yes, pointed and gold it was and always filled up with exactly 20, brand new, direct from the bank, hundred dollar bills. His friends said, "He peeled them off like toilet paper." Of course, when you use hundreds for tips like he did that many large bills are useful. But for most of us large bills are impractical except for back up in the wallet and the prosperity programming effect of the hundreds in the money clip. But Sinatra's style brings us to the question of "Just how much cash should I carry?"

"20,000 francs is a lot of money."
Bond to Tracy in *OHMSS*

You should never carry more cash than your comfort level will allow. But you should gradually increase your comfort level until you have enough cash to cover any contingency. Cash machines turn off after an earthquake, for example. So you can't always depend on the plastic in your wallet.

Also you should carry enough cash so that you'll never have to count it to see if you have enough. Remember the rich race track gambler in *Let It Ride*, who said while laughing, "Do you know how much money I have? I don't know how much money I have. That's how much money I have."

Well, that's the kind of mindset you should be in when you're carrying your cash. You can tell by the thickness of your folded cash in your pocket, with the hundred without and within, that you have enough to get you through the day, even on a luxury vacation where you're likely to be peeling many of those bills for various attractions.

Just ask yourself these questions. If I suddenly meet up with my ex-girlfriend and five of her friends and end up in a restaurant with them, do I want to worry about having enough to pay the bill? Do I want to sweat it out until the waiter tells me that they do take credit cards? Do I want to worry that there may be a glitch in their card scanner and my card won't be accepted even though I have enough credit on it? Do I want to only have a dollar left over, after paying the bill, to tip the waiter? No, you don't. You want to be able to concentrate on being a charming host, looking good in front of your ex and enjoying the time that you have with them. Assuming that you wanted to go to the restaurant in the first place. If you didn't want to go, then – loaded with cash or not – you should politely tell them the truth (that you have other plans), enjoy a few pleasantries for a moment and then head off.

Either way, this kind of situation and a host of others will come up, and will re-confirm what you already know. And that is: It's better to have cash and not need it, than to need cash and not have it.

Wayne Newton Sweats It Out

I'll further illustrate with Wayne's horror story instead of one of my own. In his younger dating days, Wayne was performing in New York and took one of the Kim sisters (three Korean singers popular at the time) out to dinner. He ended up in a Broadway Denny's restaurant with her. After finishing the main course he realized that he didn't have enough cash on him to pay the upcoming bill. Being on his first date with her he wasn't about to ask her for a loan. So he excused himself, went to the pay phone and called his brother. He explained the situation and told him to bring cash to the Broadway and Fifth Denny's restaurant. The plan being that when his brother got there he would signal to Wayne from afar and Wayne would secretly go and get the money.

To stall for time, Wayne kept the young woman entertained with conversation and dessert, all the while sweating it out waiting for his brother to arrive. To make a long horror story short, the brother was long over due and Wayne was running out of small talk and figured the girl was wondering why they were hanging around there so long. Finally an hour later, Wayne sees his brother signaling him from behind the girl at the back of the room. Feigning another trip to the restroom, Wayne went over to his brother.

"Where have you been?" Wayne asked, desperately grabbing the cash.

"Do you know how many Denny's there are in this area?" his exhausted brother asked. "Each one with three floors. There are five and I've been to all of them searching for you."

If you chuckle at this story, just put yourself in Wayne's place. Not so funny now.

Dessertless in LA

When I recorded my audio book *How to Live the James Bond Lifestyle*, my sound mixer did a great job of recording, but was not so great on listening to content. That same night he took his wife to a buffet restaurant with enough money for the food, but didn't realize that pies and cakes cost extra. Because the place was cash only, he and his wife went without dessert.

The next day at the re-mix he said to me, "I should have paid more attention to what you were saying about carrying cash than what the sound levels were."

These stories are light and humorous and no one got hurt. But you can imagine other serious situations where money could make the big difference in the safety of you and your loved ones. So carry enough cash to get the job done, be it on a date with your new Bond girl or getting your family to a safe hotel during a flash flood.

How much cash will you carry? You don't know how much cash you'll carry. That's how much cash you'll carry.

George Hamilton Learns How To Act Rich

When George Hamilton was just starting his acting career, he was hired to play a rich man. "How do I act rich?" he asked the director.

"Go to the bank and draw out five thousand dollars and put it in your pocket, then you'll feel rich and you won't have to act."

This is a good example of how carrying a lot of cash in your money clip and wallet can have an effect on you. The cash becomes a personality energizer. However, if you walk around with the fear of losing it, the cash will have the opposite effect.

As far as being robbed goes, I've heard more than one person say, after being robbed on the street, that they were very glad to have something to give the robber. That way the "transaction" was handled quickly, sending the robber on his way. I've also heard an ex-mugger say that a robber gets all worked up just before choosing his victim and making his move, so if the victim doesn't have something to give him the robber becomes super angry and then violent. So just be happy that you'll have something to give the guy if the worst should happen. And of course you'll give him all those big bills in your wallet, making him beat a happy retreat. But you'll still have the cash in your money clip to do what you have to do.

No Bond karate here please. Just survive the situation so that you can get back to your loved ones. Having said that, hopefully this will not happen to you anyway.

In his heyday with Dean Martin, Jerry Lewis would carry $3,500 around on him. I think that's way too uncomfortable, even just considering the bulk. So decide how much is comfortable for you. But remember it should be enough so that you don't have to count it to see if you have enough.

Money Has Ears

That's right. Money can hear you talking about it. And money likes to be talked nice about and likes to be handled well. Money wants respect and attention. It doesn't like to be tossed aside, ignored or taken for granted. What? Did we suddenly skip to the chapter on Bond girls? No, we're still talking about money and your relationship to it. Since money does represent energy, it does have a living quality to it. And since it's attraction to you is based on your emotionally decided financial choices, money does take on aspects of a live person, perhaps even with a female temperament. And a female wants to be treated right if she is expected to stick around and multiply.

So when you handle money, handle it with respect. Fold it gently in your money clip. Arrange it with all the presidential pictures facing the same way. Of course, when you're out in the field circulating money and getting change, you won't have time to arrange your bills so perfectly. But when you get home you should go through your money clip and reorganize them.

Never crumple money up, or stuff it clumsily into a pocket. Never say that a one, five or ten-dollar bill is small or not much money. A one-dollar bill has the power to buy some postage stamps that can send an important business or love letter to the right person that can change your life. So respect the power of even a small bill. You'll notice rich people always talk with respect for any amount of money. They realize its potential power.

Your money clip and wallet should always be put on your base of operations space with respect. Never toss them on the table. Lay them down gently.

Coming home after a day of purchases you'll have a load of pocket change. Put the pennies, nickels and dimes in a special box that is out of the way, say in a closet, and let them multiply. But don't go into that box to take them back out into the field. Take only quarters with you for your coin needs. In a couple of years you can deposit the smaller coins in your bank account.

Speaking of this you should never count out coins when making a purchase. Store clerks would rather just have the bills because it's easier to make change that way. Besides, the people in line behind you would appreciate your quick payment. Most of all you shouldn't be handling the smaller coins. Which is the reason that you put them in their own box to multiply. Sure, you must respect even the power of a penny, but you shouldn't be on that level of attention.

Your Money Body Language

Not to spy on people, but notice people's body language when paying for a purchase. Do they hold on to their money too long? Do they have a worried face when the clerk is processing their credit card? Do they have their hand out long before the clerk is ready to make change? Or is it the opposite. Do they throw their money down as if they're throwing it away with no care or respect for it? Do they crumple and stuff their change uncaringly into their wallet?

The body language that you have when paying for something will tell people a lot about you and your relationship with money. Be assured that your Bond girl will notice too. So it's important that you adjust accordingly. Look at how Bond handles money when he's paying, gambling and tipping. He handles his money with nonchalant purposeful confidence. Neither throwing it around or holding on to it too long.

The easiest money body language to spot is the hesitant body language of the 'starving student'. They will lean away from any place where they see a product for sale. They will eye a price tag with a forlorn look.

Then there is the cheap body language of a 'tight wad'. Frank Sinatra loathed cheap men and would say, "He has an impediment in his reach." Being cheap is the quickest and worst reputation to get. So while not throwing money around, be sure to have your money clip out and be peeling off your fair share of the dinner bill, including the tip.

When you're making a purchase that you have decided on, a purchase that has value to you, a purchase that is not a waste of your money, then have your cash out and ready to pay. Being a 'starving student' may be okay if you're a student, but not after you graduate from college.

"My name is James Bond. Do you take discount coupons here?"

Sounds ridiculous? Right. You don't want to be with your Bond girl at a nice restaurant and start counting out coupons in front of her and the waiter. In college, it's all right. After that, forget the coupons. It's okay to pay the fair price for something. This is not to say that you don't take advantage of bargains. But don't be doing it in the wrong place at the wrong time. The same goes with hotel bargain group clubs. Of course, become a member of the hotel chains that you use, like the Hilton Honors club. But don't get into the lower class hotel bargain groups where you're lumped together and put into bad rooms, if they happen to have the space for you. Check into a hotel with dignity, especially when you're traveling with your Bond girl, family or business associates.

Now that we've taken care of cash, for a while anyway, let's move on to another powerful prosperity technique.

"He Loves Gold. He Loves Only Gold. Only Gold"

Of course, Shirley Bassey is singing about that villain Goldfinger. Both villains and heroes can easily fall under the mysterious and attractive power of gold. Witness the 1849 California gold rush or the numerous Alaskan gold rushes. Men go crazy when they think of that shiny substance.And as mentioned before, that's what Bond carries in his briefcase for emergency funds. Gold is recognized all over the world, even in the jungles by primitive man. There's no mistaking that luster. So why not go to the precious metals dealer shop and buy a one-oz. Canadian Maple Leaf coin? About $350 should do it. Get a small flat single coin case to protect it so that you can carry it around in your pocket. Now feel the power.The next time you start running short of cash a few days before payday, you'll still feel prosperous knowing that the gold is in your pocket. If you have a real emergency, it can be quickly converted into cash. It's another way to feel like Bond.

Open a Double O Bank Account

This is a must for changing your money consciousness and upgrading your lifestyle. You already have a checking and savings account to take care of your monthly expenses. Now you need to open a 'James Bond' or 'Secret Service' account at a completely different bank.This bank should look very prosperous to you and be located in a very prosperous place. The interior should make you feel prosperous as well and the staff should make you feel comfortable. The bank doesn't have to be convenient to where you live because you won't need to go there often, especially if you handle your account by internet or direct deposit system.

This bank and this account are only for your new upgraded life, for your larger goals, your Bond trips, your new Bond car or apartment. This money is only for those items that have excitement and a 'dream' or 'luxury' image attached to them. As long as you're periodically putting money into this account, you know that you are seriously taking action on your new lifestyle. Put this bankbook in your 'treasure drawer'.

What's A Treasure Drawer?

It's just what it says. Clean out a drawer in your apartment where you can put all your financial papers and anything of real value, like your gold coin (when you're not carrying it), a small gold bar, an extra money clip holding a few hundred dollars in reserve and so on. Anything that represents value and excitement to you. Now not too much because there is always a chance that somebody will look in there and help himself to some of the items. But have enough in there so that you are impressed with it every time you open the drawer. It's a great way to program your mind. Once you have a treasure drawer started, you'll be surprised how soon it will fill up.

When the value becomes too great, you should put your treasures in a concealed place and then place the overflow into a safe deposit box in your Bond bank.

The Vacuum Technique

No, I'm not talking about cleaning up your apartment again. You've already done that, right? I'm talking about the science of creating a vacuum where the universal energy can have a place to put in more abundance for you. Nature abhors a vacuum and will do anything to fill it. So take those old clothes that you haven't worn in three years and either give them away or throw them away. You'll be surprised how fast nature will fill up your closet with the good stuff. Not only with things that you buy yourself, but 'coincidental' things, such as gifts or good finds. They will somehow magically fill your closet.

The same goes for furniture and other things. Out with the old and the new will find it's way to you. Speaking of which, never have a broken item in your home that sometimes works and sometimes doesn't. Either have it repaired or throw it out and buy another one. Broken items in your home will program you for poverty faster than anything. Fix it, replace it, or throw it out and let nature's law of filling a vacuum go into effect.

Mark This Page With a Bill

The next time you go to a bookstore, look at the bookmarks for sale near the check out desk. There are usually some that look like money. Paying real money to buy fake money? Go figure. The best type of bookmark is a crisp greenback. A real one. And this is great programming for the mind. You'll start to believe that you have an abundance of money if you can use real bills for bookmarks.

Start with a twenty and as your money consciousness moves higher, move up to a fifty and then a C note. It's especially cool to read prosperity, success and money books using a hundred-dollar bill for a marker and it's down right sacrilegious to read a Bond book with anything but.

How Do We Circulate Our Cash?

Products, services, trips, education, living space, necessities and luxuries. Which ones you choose and how much of each is up to you. Of course, having savings is very important. Being debt-free is also important and there are hundreds of money books that will tell you to save and not waste money.

However, on the other hand there are important things in life, like trips with the family, loved ones, friends and your Bond girl. The opportunities for these are not always there. So when it comes to important experiences with people that are important to you, people that are here now and may not be here later, experiences you can do while you're here and may not be able to do later, then I say: You can always work, but often an opportunity to enjoy an important experience won't come around again. Opportunities such as trips and gatherings with your parents, your high school and college graduation trip, a trip with a wonderful new relationship (that could end), or a special occasion with your children.

To repeat, savor these. Spend (circulate) your money on these. Use your credit cards if you have to and work later. I've seen countless situations where my friends (and sometimes me) missed important experiences that never came again, because they didn't want to go into debt. All of them say (including me) that they should have gone and paid it off later.

As for me, I've incurred large debts investing in my career and going on important trips with people that are important to me. In the past when I looked over my large credit card debt I did not regret any of the charges because I had gotten the value out of them. They had either moved me up slightly or largely in my career, depending on the effectiveness of that expenditure and the breaks of timing, or they were the personal trips that I mentioned. All of great value to me. All something that I would not want to erase just so as to lessen my debt.

To help me chose if I should use my credit card for that experience or investment in my career, I would use the 1 to 10 point system. 10 being the highest on my do or not scale. If it were an 8, 9, or 10 interest for me, I'd do it. And what I found out was that the thing I was considering doing was usually either a 6 or a 10. An easy choice to make. If the action I was considering was a 6, I didn't do it. If a 10, then I had no choice but to do it.

These days I have a new system. If not taking a particular action is 'not acceptable' to me, then I do it, no matter the time or expense. It's that simple. If not doing it is okay, then I don't put my energy into that.

Example: Recently my parents planned to take an overnight bus trip to Reno with a lot of their friends, friends whose company I also enjoyed. I always love casino trips with my parents. Six months before that I had missed a Mississippi River boat trip they took with their friends because my schedule couldn't match it. I wanted to make up for that and this was the opportunity to do it. It meant rescheduling my trip from Tokyo to America a month earlier, but not going on that tour was 'not acceptable' to me. So I re-arranged things so I could go. Once I made the commitment, my sister decided to go too. It was a splendid trip where I was also able to meet up with an old friend who now lives in Reno. When I saw the charge on my credit card statement, I just smiled. The thought of that trip still makes me smile.

But be careful. You have to know need from greed. You have to know if your budget can handle the extra payments to be made on your card. You have to know if the trip or event or investment in your career is really important to you or if it's just an excuse to goof off or brag to your friends about it. It could also be an excuse to hide from reality. Only you know the answer to those types of questions and whether the upcoming event that you're deciding on is a 6 or a 10.

Sammy Davis Jr.'s Lesson

On the other hand you can't go, go, go, until you're so far into debt that American Express puts Oddjob on your tail to collect from you. Yes, the party has to stop sometime and you have to go to work and pay back the money spent (circulated) on that important event.

A case in point: Sammy Davis Jr. earned and spent money on a lifestyle that included large gift giving because he admired Frank Sinatra so much that in his own words, "I wanted to be just like him." But he became overextended and in debt, so he was introduced to a new accountant who told him just what he'd have to do to get back on more stable financial ground. One of those things was to cut out the gift giving. Sammy listened intently, nodding his head all through the meeting and promised he'd turn over a new leaf. The next morning the accountant received by delivery, a Cartier gold cigarette case inscribed, "Thanks for the advice, Sammy."

Don't Buy That Carrot Juice!

Every day I buy a $2.75 cup of freshly squeezed carrot juice at a juice bar. An accountant would tell me, "Don't do that. That's $1004 a year on carrot juice. Invested at 10% that's $57,540 in 20 years. Almost $99,000 in 25 years. And $165,000 in 30 years."

"Nice idea." I'd reply. "I think I'll also stop buying toothpaste, tissue paper, mints, underwear and postage stamps. That'll save me millions over the years."

Well, you get the picture. We can't stop living. So we just have to make our choices.

A Wrist Watch Made Of Ice Cream

Recently when I wanted to upgrade to that new expensive watch that I told you about, I decided that I would use my ice cream money for it. Haagen Dazs ice cream is expensive in Japan, especially when you eat three of those small cups a day. So when I decided to circulate a lot of money for the new watch, I made a deal with myself. I would cut out the ice cream which was costing me $250 a month (I didn't want the calories anymore either) and in seven months I had a "free" Rado Ceramica watch and two inches off of my waistline.

So what does this tell us? Well, you have to choose where you want your financial energy to go. And like I said, you can't stop living, either. I will, most likely, always get my carrot juice at the juice bar instead of making it at home.

If I Win The Lottery

Everybody's favorite topic: "If I win the lottery, I will..." From now on you will never say that sentence. Because from now on you will live, think, act, walk, talk, drive, smile and take action like you've already won the lottery. This is no bull. No mind game. After all, like Charlie Sheen said to Michael Douglas in *Wall Street*, "How many yachts can you ski behind?" Well, of course the answer is one. The one that you'll rent and ski behind, if that's your dream.

Never say that energy sapping, excuse making, action-impeding sentence about winning the lottery. Sure, go ahead and buy a ticket and have fun. But act as if you've already won it. Go do what you want to do right here, right now.

I know a few people that got momentarily excited about taking action on their dreams and then bought a lottery ticket and stopped there, satisfied that they took action. Well, that's not quite enough action, is it?

Never Steal Anything Small

Or anything big, for that matter. Anytime you take something without paying for it, you are doing yourself a great disservice. It might only be a newspaper from a newsbox that was left open or a towel from a hotel, but what you are doing is telling your subconcious mind, "I can't afford this thirty-five cent newspaper or this five dollar towel. I have to steal it."

Your subconcious will accept this lack and limited thinking and impede your money circulation and your action thinking for a more prosperous lifestyle. That's how sensitive and powerful your subconcious mind is.

A Move In Vibrational Atmosphere

Here's a simple idea that I will say simply, so as to have it stick in your mind. To start upgrading your life right away, you have to get around where it's nicer. Nicer apartments, nicer restaurants, nicer movie theaters, nicer ballparks, nicer people, nicer stores and start reading nicer books. The immediate result will be that things will appear nicer automatically. They will appear and actually be nicer. Your mind will be programmed for nicer things so that you will start attracting nicer things into your experience.

Bond's Second Home

We see Bond at his apartment only once in the movie *Dr. No*. But we see him at his second home often. Where is that? When he's living at a resort hotel. Does that count as his second home? Sure it does. The operative word here is 'living'. Not buying, not owning, not selling, but 'living'.

So a big step in prosperity and 'living' like Bond is to take mental possession of all your favorite hotels. Hotels where you feel comfortable. Hotels that you've been to and enjoyed before. Hotels that you intend to go to. And any hotel in the world. Now this is not just some fun little thing to do. This is a powerful prosperity tool to use.

"But I don't own the hotel" someone might say. True enough. Which just means that you don't have the right to sell it. And you can't enjoy the pride of ownership. 'Pride' being a word we have to be careful with. Remember that the James Bond lifestyle has nothing to do with showing off or competing with friends or strangers. In fact, to move quickly up the success ladder one has to change from the competitive mind to the creative mind. If you compete with someone you stay on their level, on their wavelength, keeping you from finding your true individuality. So the 'pride of ownership' has to be eliminated from our minds. Ownership is great for the accumulation of security and wealth, to increase your vitality and productivity. However, can anything be truly owned? In two hundred years all products, cars and most buildings crumble to dust. So what do we own? Once again, only the right to sell it.

Women can accept this idea quicker than men can because they aren't into the pride part as much as men are. They love hotels because they don't have to set up and clean a hotel room like they would have to do with a second home.

So take mental ownership of hotels. You'll increase your vitality and feeling of prosperity.

The Truth About Second Homes

Ah yes, owning a cabin in the mountains. How about near Lake Tahoe? Yeah, skiing in the winter, enjoying the lake in the summer, the shows and gambling at State Line. Wouldn't owning a cabin be just great?

Well, first come up with the down payment of $30,000 and then arrange the $300,000 loan. Now you're stuck with monthly payments. And then there is insurance and maintenance. Oh, and what about worrying if someone will break in and trash it, or if someone you rent it to will trash it?

But let's say that's no problem and you're ready to visit your second home in the mountains. You take perhaps a three or four hour drive up the mountain and then you finally arrive and now you can relax. Wait a minute. Don't forget about carrying all those boxes of food and cleaning products into your cabin–the one that has sheets covering everything as dust protectors. Got to take care of those, carry them outside and shake off the dust. Next it's the broom and the vacuum cleaner. Then the clean sheets for the beds. And the rest rooms always need attention. Now take those cardboard boxes that held the food, out to the garbage. Now you can finally relax. Wait. Is that a crack in the window?

Compare that situation with this scenario: You pull up to Caesars Palace. The valet greets you and takes care of your bags and car. You check into your clean room that has soap, shampoo, towels and a freshly made bed with clean sheets, all waiting for you. Oh, is that a crack in the window? Just call the front desk and request another room. Oh, was there a snowstorm that damaged the building? Too bad, it looks like you'll have to move next door to Harrah's Hotel.

As you can see these are two different living styles. One

that requires $300,000 and a lot of work. Another that requires $150 per night and the effort it takes to pick up the room service menu.

If you already have a second or third home, great and congratulations on your prosperity. But also, take a minute to take mental possession of the hotels and other places that you want to visit. Because the final limitation of a second home is that it stays in one place. You'll always be inclined to go there for a visit. Hotels? While they don't actually move around from place to place, it feels like they do. They're always waiting there for you at any location you desire. Waiting with fresh clean rooms and ready to take your breakfast order like they did when Bond woke up in the Miami Hotel in *Goldfinger*. The golden girl kind of put a damper on breakfast, true. But we'll get to Bond girls and villains later.

To repeat: Take mental possession of all hotels. That's where Bond hangs out.

"Could you send a car to 2171 Magenta Drive?"
Bond in *Dr. No*

Take mental possession of taxis and airport vans. These are your private limos with professional drivers; ready to take you anywhere you want to go for just a few dollars and a tip. No need to buy a limo and pay the driver's salary. The same mind set as hotels comes into play here. Enough said. Think about it. Know it. Do it. Live it.

The Biggest Law Of Money

"Money, ya gotta move it around." Sinatra always said when the subject came up. And he was right. Money has to circulate. Just like electricity. Just like your blood. If you stop the flow by holding onto your money mentally, you will stop the flow of energy back to you. Therefore, you must always see the spending of money as circulatory.

The best way to visualize this is to think of yourself as a light bulb with a wire going out to a power source, such as a battery, then coming back to you on a continuing path. The wire goes out of your stomach, through the battery that is below you, then continues on around and enters your back. The faster this energy circulates the brighter you (the light bulb) shines. If you hold back the energy that goes out, the energy that comes back will quickly diminish. The same thing will happen if you hold back your friendship, love or compliments. No good energy out, nothing comes back.

In India this is called Karmic law. Simply put, the law of Karma is the natural law of cause and effect. Or as if often said in America, "What goes around comes around." Or biblically, "You reap what you sow." This is a closed universe. No energy is lost, positive or negative. There is no escaping the law of Karma.

We tend to hold on to our cash because we are constantly programmed for limitation. Just consider how products are advertised. "Hurry down while the supply lasts." "Get your seats before they're sold out." "This offer ends soon." This type of advertising plays on our fear. It takes its toll on our belief system in all sorts of ways, so we end up mentally holding onto every dollar we have and seeing the dollars that we do spend as flying away from us and never coming back.

Have you heard people say, "I hate spending money on food and rent"? This is because they have the fear that when they spend their money that it will not be coming back. Even the word 'spend' has the implied meaning of 'use up' as in all gone. So it's a good idea to use the word circulate instead of spend. As in: "I circulated twenty dollars at the restaurant." Instead of, "I spent twenty dollars at the restaurant." Yes, the subconscious mind is that sensitive. So we must always think in terms of circulating our financial energy. Never let your money mentally go away from you. Always see it as coming back.

The Power Of 10

When circulating your money, mentally attach a zero to the bills you are handing over. So that $1 is $10, $5 is $50, and so on. It's an easy thing to do. Circulate $24 and you see $240 coming back to you. This is the power of tenfold. Higher level people visualize 00 on the end of their bill that they use. But for now, it's better to keep it at one zero. You can believe 10 times is coming back to you. But to believe 100 times is coming back is difficult at the beginning. You have to build up your belief slowly for this programming technique to work.

Why We Have Limited Money Beliefs

Hundreds of years ago in Europe when the peasants out numbered the wealthy by ninety percent or more, the church and state were strongly connected. They worked hand in hand to keep the peasants from revolting. The state told the church, "We'll build you your large churches and honor your customs, but you've got to keep the peasants working the land." Thus the church emphasized Bible sayings such as, "The meek will inherit the earth" and "It is easier for a camel to go through the eye of a needle than for a rich man to enter the kingdom of heaven". "The love of money is the root of all evil". This was conveniently shortened to "Money is the root of all evil" which changed the meaning completely. The peasants were told by the church to endure the hard life and wait for their reward in heaven while the rich partied in the castle. They weren't told that Christ wore a seamless robe which was the most expensive there was. And said, "The things I do, you too can do, and even greater things."

When the Europeans came to America they brought these beliefs with them that had been passed down from generation to generation with added sayings like, "He's filthy rich," "Money is dirty," "The rich aren't happy."

Think about how people still speak about money these days. Example: When you ask for the bill for some goods or services, do you ask, "What's the damage?" As if the bill is so big and you are so poor that it will damage your financial structure.

Never say, "I can't afford it." This has a very limiting effect on the subconscious. Better to say, "I don't wish to use my financial energy on that at this time."

These limiting expressions and beliefs hold us back from attracting greater sums of money. We have to work on our minds to clear out those negative beliefs.

This is not an easy thing to do. You can say, "I am rich!" But your subconscious will come back with, "Like hell you are!" Positive thinking, speaking and affirmations don't help much. They only help a little. What are important are positive feelings and beliefs and these things can't be changed overnight. These have to grow, but there is a way to speed them along.

"Money Doesn't Grow On Trees"

When you were a kid and asked your mother to buy you a toy did she tell you, "Money doesn't grow on trees"? Mine did. But Mom was wrong, wasn't she? Because money does grow on trees, right? What's money made of? Paper. And where does paper come from? Of course, trees.

So once in a while when you pass a tree think to yourself, "What a beautiful money tree." Now maybe you'll laugh. But it will only be your conscious mind laughing. Your subconscious mind has no sense of humor and will program in anything that it hears, including the money tree.

Getting the feel of all the money trees around you is just another way of taking the financial limitations off your mind. While you're at it, any time you pass a bank be sure to acknowledge and get the feel of all that money in there. The same goes for expensive jewelry stores that you pass. Take in all of that abundance and know that there is wealth and prosperity everywhere you look. It's there for you to tap into, once you start following the rules of prosperity thinking, feeling and planning.

Later on there will be a hypnosis/meditation session that you can do yourself that will help clear your mind of negativity and free up energy that can be used to increase your financial energy circulation. But for now let's move forward to a Bond topic that will help you in all your goals, including financial.

4

THE BOND PERSONALITY

Why do we like Bond? Is it the cars? The cash? The resort hotels? The adventure? The women? Most often at my seminars I hear the words, "Because he's cool."

I think most people would agree with that, if you had to put Bond's allure in a nutshell. So what does that mean for us? We ask ourselves, "How can I be cool?" There is only one way to do it, and that way is learning to control our personality. Not have our personality control us. Most people find that concept to be a near impossible task. They say, "Hey, I'm hot headed. That's me. I can't change." They make excuses, "I've always been shy. Try as I did, I never felt comfortable in social situations."

These statements and feelings are totally human and understandable. But after we discuss the workings of the human personality and you begin to take control over it you will see some big changes in your life.

Now stick with me through here. I know this subject may not have the razzle-dazzle of the chapter on women or cash, but the upcoming ideas here will really do it for you. If you must, go ahead and flip around to other sections of the book. They are all important, useful and exciting. But please return here when you can concentrate and fully understand this chapter's techniques. This chapter will get you closer to the Bond lifestyle than any other chapter. Furthermore, it will energize all the other chapters for you. So now, having said that, let's get started.

The Mask That Covers Even 007

In the old days the Greek word for 'mask' was 'persona'. That word moved around Europe and eventually became 'personality'. The ancient Greeks seemed to know intuitively that the personality was really just a mask that we put over our true selves.

The personality consists of three energies:

1- The Body (very dense energy).

2- The Mind (mental energy) .

3- The Feelings (emotional energy).

These energies are not us. We are not our personalities. We have a body, a mind and feelings, but we are not any of these because we can control the personality. What we can control, we cannot be.

We can control our bodies. Let's test that. Put your hand up. Hold it there. Now put your hand down. Yes, you can control your body. So you are not your body.

We can control our minds. Think about *Dr. No*. Now think about Bond. Now think about Blowfeld. Yes, you can control your mind, so you are not your mind.

What about feelings? Ah yes, many people will say, "I'm

emotional. That's just the way I am and I can never control that. If someone says a bad thing to me, I just explode." However, put a $100 bill in front of that same person and tell him, "I'm going to call you all kinds of foul things and if you don't get angry for three minutes you can have the money." Now, no matter what you call him he'll control his emotions so that he can get the money. This and other similar situations prove that the feelings can be controlled. If you can control them, then you are not your feelings.

So, if you are not your personality then what are you? A human being? No, that's wrong. Oh, is that the first time you heard that you are not a human being? Once you realize this, you will move into an experience where you will gain control of all your separate energies.

So, if you are not your personality, what are you? You are perfect individualized energy. A perfect spirit. Other people have been on this planet with similar bodies, minds and feelings. But you have a unique and special energy that is totally yours alone. It was never here before and will, when you move on, never be duplicated.

Now, if you are not a human being, then what are you? You are a spiritual being going through a human evolution. That evolution is the refining of the personality. That's why when you are faced with a challenge, be it emotional, financial or physical, ask yourself, "What would James Bond do?" Then you are working on perfecting your personality. Trying to raise it to the level of perfection that your individuality is. The way to do that is to start taking gentle control over the personality. I say gentle because when you slip and make a mistake, you should not get angry or depressed about it. You should just correct yourself and try again.

Think of your personality (body, mind and feelings) as your children that you have to gently raise. And these children will make mistakes. These children will fight you for control. Especially now that you have decided to start taking control of them, which is something that you may not have been doing on a regular basis. Yes, the personality will fight you for control. But it will fight you in only two ways. And once you have identified these two ways you'll be able to see these fights coming, understand them for what they are and then handle them.

The two ways the personality fights against you are called 'personality pulls' and 'personality blocks'.

The Personality Pull

Here's an example of a personality pull. You decide that you want to lose a few pounds and save a few bucks by not buying your nightly quart of ice cream. It is the real you that makes this decision. But on the way home from work, you pass a convenience store and even though you remember your decision, you can't help going in and buying the ice cream.

You ask yourself after finishing the whole quart, "What the hell was that?" Yes, you made the decision to refrain from ice cream, but your personality pulled you toward another direction, namely the convenience store. This personality pull is aptly named, as you are pulled away from your goal.

The Personality Block

So you're in high school and you've made up your mind to ask that cute girl to the Junior Prom. You, the real you decided to do that. But every time you got near her, you got scared and didn't ask. This is an example of a personality block. The personality's fear blocked you from achieving the goal that the real you choose.

Fear is the right word for it, because there are only two energies in the universe, love and fear. Love being all the positive aspects of life: confidence, health, good money circulation, etc. Fear being on the negative side including: poverty, sickness, shyness, etc.

The personality is highly sensitive to this negative energy of fear, often crippling us and preventing us from proceeding with our mission. Your true individuality, on the other hand, is totally and completely love energy. So you don't have to add positive thinking; it's already inside you. You don't have to add money ideas; they're already inside you. You don't have to add patience. That's inside you too. All you have to do is express it.

You hear people say, "If I could only add confidence to my personality, I could accomplish more things." Again, that confidence is already inside everyone. It just has to be expressed.

Remember the song that goes, "what the world needs now is love, sweet love?" The world has all the love energy it needs. It just has to express it.

Why You Are On The Planet

You are here to raise energy, to raise the vibrational rate of your personality. That's your only job while you're visiting earth. To raise the energy of the personality to that of your spiritual individuality, which is perfect love energy. To raise the body's energy from weak to strong. To raise the mind from scattered thinking without information, to concentrated thinking and education. To raise the emotions from shy to confident, from childish to responsible. In short, to raise the imperfect personality to the perfection of the individuality.

In doing this you will come to understand that the personality has three tools (body, mind and feelings) to use to express your individuality. Your family, friends and loved ones cannot see your spirit, but you can show it to them using the tools of the personality. However, if your personality is full of fear, sickness or anger, no one will be able to see it. If your personality is relaxed and confident, you will be able to show people your true self without it being blocked by the personality. This is the reason that James Bond is so cool. He has his personality under control.

To clarify, think about a dancer or athlete. When they are 'in the zone,' when their minds and feelings are relaxed yet concentrated, they can show us their true individuality and spirituality by using their bodies which flow from movement to movement in a splendid, graceful manner. However, if they're angry, shy or in poor health, their personality's problems block out their spirituality and we see only the imperfect human.

A nurse, a mother or a lover would use their feelings to show their true selves. A teacher, speaker or writer, if they are not blocked with fear or anger, can express their individuality using their mental energy.

So raising the vibrational rate of energy is your only job. To go from Barney Fife to James Bond, if you will. From an emotionally out of control person to one that is in control. And do not think that gaining control of your feelings will make you an unfeeling robot. On the contrary, when you free up your emotions, you can strongly feel what you want to feel when you want to feel it.

Someone might ask, "Is all this self-attention and education being selfish?" No, not at all. Because once you have moved up the energy of the personality you can then pass this energy to others. (Only if they ask. Not by intrusion.) Then later maybe you can add to the world's energy by making a global contribution, like feeding a foster child, saving plant or animal life, or adding to the education of the world.

However, you can't give success away unless you have it yourself. You can't give money away unless you have it yourself. You can't educate anyone unless you have information to give. It's the old joke: What do you need to know to teach a dog? More than the dog.

Many parents will say, "My family comes first." But, and I know this will sound anti-traditional, you must take care of your own energy first. This doesn't mean that you run off to the library or gym for 18 hours a day and neglect everyone. This means that you get enough sleep, nutrition and an hour a day to satisfy your emotional needs or whatever your private time relaxations are.

Take care of yourself first and the other relationships will flow more smoothly. The main reason relationships don't run smoothly is that the people are not taking care of themselves first. The I'll-take-care-of-you idea is now changing. Some understand a certain virtue in being selfish: You take care of yourself for me and I'll take care of myself for you.

Any child psychologist will tell you that the worst thing for a child is the unsatisfied parent. The child, no matter the age, can feel the parent's frustration and unhappiness. Nobody can fully enjoy a friend, lover or parent that is sick, sleepy, angry, frustrated, broke or unenlightened. Even airline emergency instructions tell you to put on your oxygen mask first before putting on your child's mask. You can't help them if you're out cold.

To repeat, your first responsibility is to take care of and raise up your own personality (body, mind and feelings) first.

It's In The Vibes. Good Vibes. Bad Vibes.

As you learned in 7th grade science class, everything in the world is vibrating. The law of physics says that like vibrations attract. Unlike vibrations don't do too well together. For example, when a high-tension wire touches a low-tension wire, the low-tension wire breaks. When the vibrations in your life are too severely different, things become painful. When you put your foot, that is vibrating slowly, into hot bath water that is vibrating fast, there is pain until your foot gets used to the hot water by raising its vibration to that of the hot water.

Pain caused by differences in vibrations is a good thing. If you are talking and absentmindedly put your hand out behind you into a fire, the pain that follows is good. It tells you to move your hand. If there were no pain, your hand would burn up unnoticed by you. Likewise, boredom is a good source of pain, for a short while. If you're bored at your job, this is the higher intelligence in your mind calling up to you and saying, "It's time to find a more creative and fulfilling job." If there is pain in a love relationship, you're being told to repair the situation or move on. That's why pain, for a short while, is useful if it makes you take action and moves you forward with your life.

To repeat, this is a closed universe and no energy escapes. We are walking around in a sea of energy, but we don't know it. Just like fish in the water. They don't know they are in the water because that's what they live in naturally. If a muddy fish comes into a goldfish bowl, its mud will float around and contaminate the water and then the other fish. If you are in a room talking high-energy ideas with a friend and someone enters that is negative and dark, without even seeing him, you will feel the 'bad vibes' flowing into you. They will make you feel uncomfortable, because of their lower vibration. Just as extreme heat or cold makes you uncomfortable.

Likewise, the low vibrational person is not comfortable in a room where there are high-energy conversations or vibrations. That is why successful people hang out with other successful people and negative people hang out with other negative people. Because like vibrations are comfortable. These vibrations are transmitted out of your body producing an aura. That's why lovers don't even have to touch to get excited. Just by sitting near each other, they feel each other's energy.

An example of this is the tuning fork. If you hit one tuning fork so that it will vibrate and then put another tuning fork near it, that one will start vibrating 'in sympathy' with the other just by feeling the vibrations through the air.

By the way, when a friend is having a problem you should never lower your energy and give that person 'sympathy'. This will only increase your friend's bad feeling and bring you down, too. So don't vibrate 'in sympathy' with your distressed friend. Instead, give your friend understanding and help, by keeping your vibrational energy up and lending support. This is not to say that you approach your friend with a crazy 'positive attitude' as if everything is great. This means being a good listener and offering constructive advice or just being there. But to repeat, keep you vibrational energy up. You'll do more good that way.

So what do all these scientific energy rules have to do with living the James Bond lifestyle? It has everything to do with it. In order to attract more money, you must first raise up your mental and emotional vibrations concerning money.

Also remember that a nicer apartment and nicer hotels also have a higher vibrational rate. And, as mentioned before, so do positive words, healthy food, classic literature and so on. Once again, to move forward you have to get around where it's nicer.

Higher Vibrational Food

Now that you've seriously considered the 007 lifestyle you should consider stepping up your body's maintenance program. The good news is that this will become automatic as you move to a higher vibrational rate of thinking and feeling.

Food has vibration rates as well as everything in life. And, to repeat, the law of life is that same vibrations attract. So as you get more organized, value your time more, control the negative thoughts, avoid negative people and places and pursue your dreams, you will find that your eating habits will naturally improve.

In fact, as a society matures, its eating habits improve. All the menus from the presidential inauguration parties are still available for viewing. If you look at the first years you'll see it's mostly meats with very few vegetables. Every twenty years or so the menu changes and is healthier. When you look at recent years, you'll see just one meat selection, while the bulk of the menu is vegetables and fruit. As America's vibration as a whole improved, so did the vibration of the inaugural menu.

So improve your lifestyle and the food and exercise will follow suit. But while you're waiting for that to happen, it won't hurt to put some energy forth and start eating well and getting some exercise.

The Body Of A Double O Agent

The James Bond lifestyle requires almost by definition that you be healthy. That's why I suggested that one of your magazine selections should be concerned with health. There is so much material on health that you'll have to dig into it yourself if you want to go deeper. I've read volumes on the subject coming from a variety of respected health experts. The following seems to be a must to keep the body serving you while both on a field mission, at your base of operations, or at a resort.

Water: Drink a lot of filtered water. Your body is seventy percent water and your brain is eighty percent water. Doctors that specialize in the body's need for water say that all the functions of brain and body are enhanced when they're properly hydrated.

Food: Likewise, seventy percent of your food should be water-based fruits and vegetables. Cut down on or cut out; dairy products, egg yolks, beef, pasta, bread and wheat products.

Avoid These Things

Beef: Animal digestive tracts are made for beef because the beef moves through them in an hour. The human digestive tract takes four hours for food to move through. The digestive tract is very warm. What would happen if you leave beef out on the table on a warm day for four hours? It would putrefy. That's what's happening to it in your body.

Nicotine: Bond quit smoking in *The World Is Not Enough*. ("Filthy habit," he says in the movie.) That should be a sufficient motivator if you're serious about this course.

Caffeine: It's in coffee, cola and chocolate. Cut it way down.

Sugar: Americans have cut down their fat intake, but their weight increases. Why? Sugar is what the experts say. But don't replace sugar with any 'sugar free' food such as diet colas. There are bad chemicals in those. If you must drink colas, drink the real stuff.

Alcohol: Shake it, don't stir it, but don't swallow much of it. Alcohol impedes mission success.

A good way to think about nutrition is: If you had a million dollar race horse would you feed him candy bars, potato chips, coffee and donuts? Not if you wanted him to finish in the money you wouldn't. Well, your body is worth more than a million dollars because no amount of money can replace it. So start giving you body the kind of nutrition that it deserves so that it can finish in the money every day.

Exercise

Long time health guru Jack LaLane says, "The reason that you can't do what you used to do, is because you stopped doing it." Meaning, you used to be able to swim 20 laps in the pool, but now you can't because you stopped swimming. So it's time to get back to it.

Walking and stair climbing win the safe and effective vote, with all forms of exercise being beneficial. Just be sure to take care of both the muscular and cardiovascular systems of your body.

Sleep

Sleep specialists say that the human body needs eight hours of sleep. If you sleep less than that you incur a 'sleep debt' that must be paid back to maintain proper heath, top energy and concentration. Every night that you don't sleep eight hours your sleep debt increases. It must finally be paid back with a long sleep or with 'power naps'.

If you think about it, you never saw Bond yawn. And any woman will tell you that one of the worst things you can do with her on a date is yawn. Nobody, man or woman, wants to date a zombie. The walking dead are just no fun at all. They fall asleep in theaters, parties and even on amusement park rides. I heard of one guy on a date falling asleep in Disneyland's Haunted Mansion. I guess being a zombie, he felt at home there and decided to take a power nap. His girl is probably dating some live guy now.

Turn Your Body's Health Over to Your Subconscious

Don't worry so much about the separate functions of your body. Let the higher intelligence in you take care of that. The body's natural tendency is to go towards health. When you cut your finger, you put a Band-Aid over it, but then the body heals itself. When you break a bone the doctor sets it and then the body repairs the bone. Always go to a medical doctor first and then let the body do its work, aided by your positive thinking and feeling.

When you are healthy, aid the body to stay that way with good food, exercise, rest and a positive mind. Some people believe that it's natural to be sick, but don't fall into that mind set. The fact is that it's natural to be healthy. And always remember to talk about health, not about sickness. That's how sensitive the mind is.

The Mind of a Good Field Agent

When Bond goes out in the field he has to keep his mind focused on one thing, the mission. When he loses that concentration, like he did at Blowfeld's Piz Gloria base in *OHMSS* when he started messing with the girls, he ends up in big trouble.

When George Sidney was directing *Pal Joey* he said to Frank Sinatra, "Frank, you're making movies, recording, performing, running the world. How do you do it?"

Sinatra answered,"I concentrate on one thing at a time."

Concentration. That's the ticket. But often we are distracted from our purpose, like Bond sometimes is. But who can blame him when he's cooped up on a mountaintop with a smorgasbord of women. Well, we can't blame him, but look what happened – a close brush with failure.

What happens to us when we are distracted? It is usually fear that takes away our concentration. This usually manifests itself with either worry or anger. Consider this situation:

You've purchased tickets to see your favorite singer in concert. Expensive tickets, that you bought two months in advance, with the hopes of finding a cool girl to take there with you. Then you do meet someone who may become special and she accepts your invitation to go to the concert. "Wow! This is great," you think. "Great seats to see my favorite singer and a great date to take as well."

The night of the concert comes and you decide to take a taxi to the concert to avoid the congested parking. On t he way, the driver starts mouthing off, giving you and your date all kinds of foul opinions of the world, then he verbally attacks you for seeing this "low life singer," and then tells your date that she "shouldn't be with a jerk like you." When you don't have the exact change he starts yelling and swearing at you until you tell him to keep the change of a fifty for a twenty-dollar ride.

Now you're sitting in the concert, in those great seats, with your favorite singer doing your very favorite songs and your dream date is sitting next to you. All you do is think of that S.O.B. taxi driver. You want to enjoy the concert and your date. Yes, you do. The real you wants to. But your mind keeps replaying the taxi driver incident so loudly that you can't seem to even hear the singer and you don't even care that your date seems interested in you. What's happening? And what can you do about it?

Mentioned earlier, controlling the emotions will let you feel what you want to feel when you want to feel it. Likewise, by controlling the mind you can concentrate on what you want to at the moment. These images of the taxi driver keep coming back into your mind with feelings of anger attached to them are distracting you from your goal of enjoying the concert and your date to the fullest.

These negative thoughts about the taxi driver are real electrical charges in your brain that feed off and want mental and emotional attention and energy. Just like if you give a stray cat milk outside your door one night. What will happen the next night? He will return and start crying again for more milk, more energy. The more you feed it, the more frequently and quickly it will return and he'll return also with more stray cats for you to give milk to. That's what's happening with these negative taxi driver thoughts. They want mental energy. Mental 'milk' if you will.

So use the technique of seeing these mental nuisances as stray cats that come into your brain seeking 'milk'. Now, say to that cat, "Not now, I'm enjoying the concert." And give them a mental push with your hand, out of your brain. When they come back again a minute later, repeat the words and the action of pushing them out. "Not now, I'm enjoying the concert." Soon they will stay out.

After the concert is over and your date is safely home, you can return to your apartment and then get angry at that taxi driver and get it out of your system. Now that's mind control. That's controlling your emotions.

Never forget about all the power that is in your mind and feelings. Be careful not to give it away to low energy jerks like that taxi driver. Why should you give your power over to them? Of course, it's natural that you release the negative energy or else you end up like Robert De Niro's character in *Taxi Driver* with a Mohawk, talking to yourself in the mirror. That's why we say, "Asshole" when someone cuts us off in traffic. Or think, "Son of a bitch," when some guy steps on our toe on a crowded bus. When that happens to me on the crowded trains in Japan, I remember the lady in the original *King Kong* who has her foot stepped on as a man moves past her. She says in effect, "Gee, ain't we got enough gorillas in New York." That dispels my negative annoyance and humors my mind, without giving too much power away to some insensitive clod who is stomping around a crowded train instead of doing the 'sliding shuffle' that others do, so as to not step on toes.

Assholes, Sons-of-Bitches and Jerks

By calling a guy an 'asshole' or 'son of a bitch' in your mind, you are giving him too much power over you. And you're programming your mind that you are a victim. But yes, the annoyance has to be dissipated in your mind somehow, so what can you do? Well, why don't you change the word 'asshole' or 'son of a bitch' to 'jerk'? A jerk is an insensitive guy who doesn't realize where he's at or what he's doing, nor understands or cares that he's affected someone negatively. His attacks aren't so directed against people. Thus you can dispel your anger with a lighter word.

I've used the word 'jerk' for a long time, but have

recently starting using one that humors me more. It's the name 'Clyde'. Frank Sinatra and his Rat Pack, to signify a 'square' used Clyde -someone who wasn't 'hip' or 'with it'. A Clyde was a cheap guy who never tipped. A Clyde was a guy who wore brown shoes after dark. (Sinatra would tell people, "What the hell are you wearing brown shoes after dark for? Go change them.") This makes me laugh. Both at Sinatra's strict dress code and at the poor 'Clyde' that had to go change his shoes. So now when a guy cuts me off in traffic, blocks the entrance to a door and so on, I just think, "What a Clyde. He probably wears brown shoes after dark."

This not only makes me chuckle inside, but equates me a little with Sinatra and dispels my annoyance so that I can forget that 'son of a bitch' as soon as possible. So why not give 'Clyde' a shot and use it for those 'Assholes'. Clyde isn't heard much these days and maybe we should keep it alive for the sake of 'the pack'.

But if you must go Bond all the way, the next time some Clyde cuts you off in traffic, just say to him in your mind what Bond said to villain Donald Grant in *From Russia with Love*, "What lunatic asylum did they get you out of?"

Reread these mental techniques and start to put them in action to control that part of your personality. It's a must if you want to become Bond cool.

"You forget, I took a first in oriental languages at Cambridge."
Bond to Moneypenny in *You Only Live Twice*

You have to feed the mind to grow. You'll notice that James Bond is well educated. Every time M asks him if he knows about something, he knows a lot about it. So Bond is well read and he retains what he reads.

A very important part of the James Bond lifestyle is to constantly study. Always have a book you're reading near your mission control center. And not just for the sake of it. Find out what you're interested in and study it. Naturally, you're interested in increasing your lifestyle, so more books and seminars on this subject will be of interest to you. Then hit the bookstores and libraries to find more information on the subject.

Also study your chosen profession. Make yourself more valuable in the market place. Of course, you are a valuable person, a valuable family member and a valuable community member. But you also need a marketable skill that you can sell to be valuable in the job market.

"You are unusually well informed, Mr. Bond"
Auric Goldfinger

A great innovation for education in the past 20 years has been the cassette tape. Self help books, modern fiction, history, science and many of the classics are on cassette tape. You can listen in the car and at home, making your study choice entertaining instead of painful.

You should have three classics that you know well. Find a few novels that you are interested in and buy the audio books. Listen to them a couple of times through. And then buy the 'Cliff Notes' on those novels. These are written by professors that specialize in teaching those novels and will have clarifications of all of its aspects. This way you won't be left out of the conversation when the subject goes from your favorite movies to your favorite novels.

With my love of movies, naturally I'm attracted to novels that were made into some good movies. Here are some suggestions if you lean that way, too.

The Time Machine by H.G.Wells
(Only 100 pages, or 3 hours on tape)
The Strange Case of Dr. Jekyl and Mr. Hyde by Robert Louis Stevenson (100 pages)
Moby Dick by Herman Melville
(Long, but considered to be America's best novel.)
Crime and Punishment by Fyodor Dostoyevsky
Les Miserables by Victor Hugo
Frankenstein by Mary Shelley (She wrote it when she was 18, so don't say you're too young to do something special.)
The Picture Of Dorian Gray by Oscar Wilde (This is not only my favorite; Alfred Hitchcock also called this his favorite book.)

These are my favorites, but you should choose your own and study like Bond. These higher level writings will help your thinking, vocabulary and give you a connection to history as well.

So feed that all-important part of your personality, the mind. One day you might tell someone, "You forget, I took a first in American Lit at MYU (my alma mater)."

Bond Cries For Tracy in OHMSS

The feelings. What a mystery they are. They made even Bond cry. Of course, it was the right time to cry. And Bond felt what he wanted to feel, at that sad time.

The feelings are the hardest of the personality's energies to control. But as mentioned before, it can be done. It must be done to have a successful mission and accomplish your goals. Whether the goal is business, education, travel, or romantic in nature. For example, 'the green eyed monster' namely jealousy, has destroyed many a love relationship. Until we start taking gentle command over the emotions, we cannot move forward quickly in our lives, without having the negative emotions sabotage us at the last minute and destroy all the work we've done up to that point.

Our feelings are actually part of our subconscious energy. They form our belief structure. An image linked to a feeling gives us our beliefs. These beliefs are often limited in nature and put a barrier on what we are trying to accomplish. They also impede the speed at which we can accomplish things. Thus, changing our feelings at a deep subconscious level and taking off these limitations is all-important.

To work with our feelings is to work with our subconscious mind. So let's move forward to that.

The Subconscious Mind

Stronger than any gadget that you can get from Q branch is your own mind. It's often said that we use only ten percent of our brain. Now I'd like to introduce you to the other ninety percent. Namely your subconscious mind. This is the part of your mind that never sleeps. The part that controls your bodily functions when you're sleeping. This is your feeling energy that is not only in your brain, but flows throughout your entire body. And it works in a very particular way.

Think of your conscious mind as a PC keyboard that is controlled by you and can make decisions. Think of your subconscious as the floppy disc that accepts the programs you enter. Whatever you enter. Ah, there's the rub. It will accept anything that you enter into it, but we aren't always aware that we're doing it. That's why it is of the utmost importance to start a healthy relationship with this 'best friend' or 'worst enemy' of yours. Because once this programming is accepted by the subconscious, it will go about trying to bring into manifestation the programming you give it.

For this keyboard/floppy disc analogy there is one problem. The enter key is not hit by you. The enter key is always on. The programming vehicle is an image with a feeling attached to it. The stronger the image and especially the feeling, the stronger the programming. The more the image and feeling are repeated, the stronger the mind will be imprinted with that program. So the problem is that if you're in a negative mood with negative thoughts and feelings, your subconscious is taking this all in and setting up negative programs.

However, the sort of good news is that when your energy is up and positive, with images of success, this is being accepted into your mind as well. The reason I say "sort of good news" is that the mind will believe and accept the negative ten times faster than it will believe and accept the positive. This is because we are constantly bombarded with the negative and, after all, this is a world of inertia and resistance, so in fact, it does take a lot of energy to bring your goals into reality, thus the slowness in believing the positive.

Another problem is that ninety percent of images and words we see and hear are negative. Just pay attention to the evening news or the way people communicate. In fact, the first thing that happens when you start getting into this kind of teaching is that you notice how negatively people talk. Most people will tell you what they're "coming down with" instead of what they're "coming up with." Examples are: "I'm sick and tired of this," "I'm dead tired," "I'm dead broke," "I'm having a bad day," "He'll be the death of me," "He's a pain in the ass," and so on.

It is said that a child hears the word "No" ten times more than the word "Yes". That's a lot of negative programming at an age when the mind is super sensitive. It is now known that an individual's personality is ninety percent formed by the age of three. That's something to think about when raising a child.

Later, in an upcoming chapter we'll talk about how negative advice based on fear or jealousy can program you right out of your mission and dreams.

Of course, the strongest of the mind programmers are the advertisers. They understand full well the workings of the subconscious mind to program you to buy their product. Exciting music on TV commercials is played to excite your emotions with the image of the product being flashed. This is repeated throughout the week. Emotions plus image plus repetition equals a programmed mind or 'brainwashing'. If you don't want to receive the programming, say or think the word "erase". This will protect you somewhat, but not completely.

A way to think about your protection system is to think that there is a small doorway from your conscious mind to the subconscious. At that doorway is a little version of you standing guard. When you hear or see a negative thing, close the door and don't let the programming in. When there are positive images that benefit you, let the door open and say, "Yes, program that."

This is not to say that you hide from the world, news information or constructive criticism. But any psychologist will tell you that the insecure man will see garbage on the street that has nothing to do with his life, walk up to it and say, "I can deal with this garbage." This is because of his masculine pride. It's the very secure man that glances at it and says, "This is not part of my life and I don't want to deal with it." (Of course, if the garbage is dumped on his front lawn he has to deal with it.) So choose for yourself what garbage you have to deal with and what negative garbage has no place in your life.

The Power Of Words

Nothing escapes your subconscious mind. The thing to remember is that your subconscious has no sense of humor. Even a joke that is not meant to be taken literally, will be received that way by your subconscious. "If it weren't for bad luck, I'd have no luck at all." This may be funny to the conscious mind, but a true and potent statement to the subconscious. Your subconscious is ready to be programmed, so try to avoid any negative statements about yourself, even humorous ones.

Speaking of word power, did you know that when your vocabulary goes up, your IQ goes up as well? Start using higher vibrational words in your communication. Not to impress others, but to impress your mind with a higher power vocabulary.

The Two Most Powerful Words

"I'm happy." "I'm broke." "I'm sick and tired." "I'm a mess." "I'm prosperous." Can you find the two most powerful words among these? They are the words, "I am." These two words will program the mind more than any others. And what you put after them will become your life. "I am ________." Just fill in the blank and your mind will start guiding you to that state of being, whether it's positive or negative. It will just follow your orders. Like the genie in the lamp, it will do your bidding with the magic words of "I am ______." or the contraction "I'm _______." Start to edit your speech when you catch yourself putting in negative words into the blank. Say "erase" and then put in a positive word in its place. Are you ready to do that? Just fill in the blank and that will be your life. "I am _______."

The Year Cycle And The Birth Cycle

The subconscious mind is very sensitive to the new year. It understands the feeling of a new beginning. Whatever you are thinking and feeling as you go into the New Year is strongly programmed into your mind and will start attracting those images into you life with more power than other times in the year. So care must be taken as to what one is thinking and feeling as the new year rolls around.

It's interesting to note that in Japan, it's the new year custom for a person to clean up the entire home and then at midnight go to a temple to pray for a prosperous year. Some temples have large bonfires where you can throw a few coins into a box (evoking the law of circulation) and then throw any unneeded things into the large fire, such as last year's calendar. Thus, further programming the mind that the old is finished and the new is here, hopefully with a higher way of feeling and thinking.

Unfortunately, in America many people go into the new year semi-conscious (drunk), missing the opportunity for programming in a clear plan for that year. In fact, they are programming in an uncertain and unfocused new year.

A person's birthday is a similarly powerful time for programming the mind and beginning a fresh new cycle. So as you can see, we have two chances a year to let the old, unwanted items and thinking fade back and let the new thinking come in with energetic expectation.

Before every new year and every birthday, I recommend cleaning up your apartment, getting rid of old papers and items, making a list of goals for that new birth cycle and getting yourself a birthday or new year's gift such as a success book. Put that new book on your mission planning space as an energizer and get ready for new action, more prosperity and more manifestations of your dreams. Never let a birthday or new year go by unnoticed.

Levels of Programming

Everything that has ever happened to you is recorded in your mind. If you'll imagine ten levels where these incidents are recorded depending on the intensity of them, you'll get the idea of how the brain stores memory. Unimportant things will be recorded at a lower level and you won't remember them, but they are there. Intensely happy or traumatic incidents will be recorded on a higher level. This is important to understand, as these levels have to be cleansed of the negative feeling energy that is attached to the images of your past experiences. Later in this book, there will be a hypnosis session printed for clearing the subconscious mind of these negative feelings. But for now, just be aware of the power and the recording capabilities of your mind.

Belief Is Essential To Get Your Mission Completed

Another way of explaining the subconscious is that it is your belief system. You have beliefs that have been programmed into you since birth. Warm is good. Milk is great. The doctor's office is bad. Then as you get older opinions of others are programmed into you. For example: Money is hard to make. It takes money to make money. You'll never amount to anything. You're a loser. Only famous people can get published. And so on.

If a person doesn't believe he can accomplish something, he'll never try. If his subconscious believes that he doesn't deserve success or if his subconscious buys into the negativity that it creates, he will subconsciously sabotage himself on the way to his goals. This happens with negative self-talk. For example, "If I become successful, I'll lose my friends." Just as he gets to the point where he has the contract for that next project or job in his hand, he'll find a way to destroy it. This usually happens by him inventing a problem and starting an argument with the very person that is handing him the opportunity.

When I heard of this idea, I couldn't really believe that someone might throw away success when they're so close to it. But then I saw it on a movie project that I was working on. It's pretty scary to witness and the problem is that if you're associated with that person or project you get dumped right along with him. "Why did you start yelling at the very man who was going to finance the movie?" I asked the guy after the financier changed his mind and left the room.

"Well, I had to express my true feelings," he told me. He got to express his feelings and put him and everyone who had worked to get this project started, out of work.

"Don't worry," he said. "There are other money men out there."

I saw him continue to search for production money after that, but he never was able to put a project of any type together. He moved from one friend's house to another, wearing out his welcome, leaving behind a large phone bill and then finally disappearing from the film-making scene altogether. At the time I didn't understand it. But after studying psychology more and seeing other examples first hand, I came to believe it.

This will not happen to you because you will program yourself to do what is necessary, whatever is necessary to get your goals accomplished. You won't "have to break some eggs to make an omelet." This phrase is use by people who need an excuse to treat people unfairly as they ruthlessly strive for the top. You'll know that this type of behavior is not necessary once you start reading more books written by successful businessmen. Fair play and win/win negotiations will get you where you want to go and help you stay there, faster than stepping on people and friends.

But don't be mistaken about this type of teaching. It's not about being positive and skipping through the flowers and saying, "Everything is beautiful and here Mr. Robber take my wallet." No, it's not about that. Nature is overall perfect. The weather is overall perfect. But sometimes the rain comes and sometimes the wind comes. When you are experiencing a particularly low cycle in your life, either personal or business, this teaching will help you make it through those tough times.

So take some time alone to think about how you feel about going after and achieving your goals. How you feel about taking action on upgrading your life. Are you comfortable with the idea of it? Can you handle the extra work, the extra responsibility and the extra risk? Are you worried about some of your friends becoming jealous and perhaps trying to sabotage you or talk you out of your action? It will happen. But that will be a signal that you are on the right track.

I found out the hard way that you can't take people along with you that don't have the belief or want the responsibility. No matter how much you want them to be successful with you, they will drop out before moving up to a level that feels mentally and emotionally uncomfortable to them. This is because the higher vibrations of the goal you're going after are too much for them. But these higher vibrations won't be too much for you, if you keep your belief high and move forward 'testing the waters' as you go.

When Bond Goes Out On A Mission He Is Attacked

Yes, he is. Always. That's a law of life. Any forward action will be attacked from without and perhaps from within. That's to be expected. And that's the answer that you give yourself when you say, "Why did this guy attack my project?" He attacked because that's the way things are set up on the planet. If you plant a corn field, right when the corn is about to mature so that you can take it to market, the crows come, the insects come, the thieves come. And maybe a couple of your farm hands will go out at night and set fire to your crop just because they thought it would be fun, even though you've been paying them a higher than usual salary. That's just the way it is and you'll have to understand it and protect yourself from it as best you can.

Actor Michael Caine said, "When you're wealthy, you have to protect yourself from certain people that you might make the mistake of inviting into your house. They'll steal from you. They'll even take the pillow cases."

Now that you're embarking on living the lifestyle of 007 you'll see these attacks coming right away. "What are you dressed up for?" "What are you going to night school for?" "Oh, were those important papers of yours that I threw out?" Don't get negative or cynical, but look out for the attacks.

Remind yourself often that, "I am not a human being. I am a spiritual being going through a human evolution. I am here on this planet to increase the energy of my personality and to perfect my individuality. I will now take gentle control over my personality."

These words should easily ring true to you and keep you cool and prepared for the upcoming attacks. This understanding of not being a human being, but a spiritual being, is the most important concept needed to become cool like Mr. Bond.

Never Breathe a Sigh of Relief

That sounds like a title for a Bond movie doesn't it? What this is actually referring to is this: Anytime you finish a fearful or tense situation, when you breathe out a sigh and say to yourself, "I'm glad that's over with," you are setting yourself up for another fearful situation.

For example, maybe you're not too keen on flying and when you get out of the plane you breathe a sigh of relief. What you are inadvertently telling your subconscious is that this is a fearful situation to be wary of. So the next time you're in an airplane you'll have a repetition of that fear and maybe even experience a stronger one.

What you should do when you get off of the plane is to think to yourself with feeling, "I loved that plane ride. I wish I were still on that great wonderful airplane, because I love to fly. That's right, I love to fly."

Of course, you will know that is BS, but your subconscious believes anything you tell it with feeling and repetition, so it will reduce the fear the next time you fly.

You should do this after any fearful situation that you have. So the next time that you catch yourself giving out a sigh of relief, quickly reverse the fearful programming to a new image of relaxation and confidence to lessen the fear, or perhaps eliminate it, the next time that same experience happens.

Sammy Meets The Queen

When Sammy Davis Jr. met Queen Elizabeth II during a receiving line, he was understandably nervous. He wasn't sure if he should put out his hand first or not. When she approached, he quickly stuck out his hand, then retracted it. The Queen had stuck out her hand, but then retracted it also. Seeing the Queen with her hand out, Sammy stuck out his and, but then retracted it again. After the third time of this routine, the Queen grabbed his hand quickly with both her hands to stop this embarrassing display.

We've all been in these social situations where we are unsure as what to do. Going to many social gatherings in Japan, I've often been unsure of what the customs dictate in certain social situations. But I soon discovered the secret of how to handle the scene.

Instead of nervously taking quick action and hoping it's the proper move, I slow my mind and body movements way down and let the action of the situation move me as to what to do, where to sit, when to speak. If I met the Queen I would go into my slow motion mode and let her words and movements guide me.

So any time you're in an intimidating social situation, go into the slow motion mode and sit where they tell you to sit, use the fork that everyone else picks up and applaud when everyone else does. This is much easier than nervously darting around the room like Barney Fife or Woody Allen trying too hard and too fast to figure out what to do.

So click into the slow motion mode during those intimidating situations and be James Bond cool.

Now that we've addressed the inner you, let's move forward and address the outer you.

5

YOUR APPEARANCE

The Bond Face

The very first mistake most guys make when they try to emulate 007 is that they start wearing a tough guy grimace, accompanied by a deadly stare, with a professional wrestler's swagger. Nothing could be further from the truth. If you look at all the actors that played Bond, you'll see that they have a relaxed, easygoing expression on their faces, with a light smooth walk to match. Notice in *OHMSS* how George Lazenby as Bond walks down the hotel stairs and into the casino. He moves casually and happily as he glances around with an interested warm demeanor.

A notable thing to remember here is that an interesting face is more attractive than just a handsome face. Repeat: An interesting face is more attractive than just a handsome face, or a pretty face for that matter. How do you have an interesting face? Be interested.

When walking through an airport, hotel, or shopping mall, take in the atmosphere. Be interested in what's going on. Not in a tourist gawking pointing around way, of course, but with a mental attitude of, "Well, isn't this an interesting place."

With those words in your mind and a few slight glances around, you'll have an expression that says 'I'm interested.' This way you'll make a better impression than a really handsome guy who has a stoic or mean expression on his face. So cut out the 'kill you' face. That's only in the action scenes.

If the 'be interested' mind set doesn't work for you consider this. The next time you're walking through the mall pretend your ex-girlfriend is watching you from a distance. I'm sure you'd want her to see in your face and walk a prosperous interested person who just came from some interesting place and is headed to another interesting place (maybe a rendezvous with a Bond girl). You don't want your ex to see you walking downtrodden through the world as if your breakup with her has made you a broken man.

At my seminars, this idea really strikes home especially to the male ego. So, "Here I am walking through this cool mall, checking things out, with a hint of a smile on my face that tells the whole story after the break up of how well I'm doing. Now if I had just remembered to put on some better clothes." Ah yes. What would Bond be wearing at this time, place and occasion (the old T.P.O.)?

Face Programming

You've heard the saying; "You earn the face you get at forty." The reason that is true is that the subconscious mind programs the one hundred and twenty muscles of your face with every thought and feeling you have. When a person is forty those muscles become permanent. They have shaped themselves into those thoughts and feelings, showing on his face what is in his mind and heart. (The word heart was first used for the idea of a person's true deep feelings, before the word subconscious came about.)

In many cultures it is often noticed that a husband and wife start to look like each other after twenty years of marriage. The simple truth of the matter is that they do because they have been living in the same house with the same vibrational situation. If it's a happy house, the two of them will have happy faces. If it is a house of tension and bickering, that will also affect both of their faces.

So control your thoughts and feelings. Don't let the dark ones stay long enough to start messing with your face and encourage the happier ones.

The Healthy Sun Tan

Sure a sun-tanned face looks healthy. It also looks prosperous, as if you've had lots of leisure time playing tennis, golf, or hanging around a resort pool. But with the ozone layer thinning out these days, the incidence of skin cancer is increasing, even with sunblock. "The problem with sun block," says skin specialist Dr. Marvin Engel, "is that it gives sun worshipers a false sense of security."

So protect yourself from the sun, which you'll be out in more than before now that you have committed yourself to living like 007. This means you will be hitting the resorts and amusement parks and this also means that the sun will be hitting you. So use a well-known effective brand of sun block with a high SPF. On top of that wear a hat and a long sleeve shirt when walking around for periods over twenty minutes. Be sure to especially protect your nose, which gets more than its fair share of the sun. Also don't forget that water reflects the sun giving you a double dose when you're on a boat or by the pool.

Now about that healthy suntan. It's best to get it out of

a bottle. Bronzing gel for men is just the ticket. Try out some well-known brands and experiment with the colors and application. It only takes a minute in front of the mirror. A lot of bronzers have sun block in them, which will help protect your skin as well.

So protect your skin at all costs. And remember leather makers put animal skins outside in the sun so that they become dried out, tough and hard. This process is called 'tanning'.

"No well dressed man should be without one."
Bond taking off his jetpack in *Thunderball*

Before going out in the field where one might need a jetpack, let's consider what Bond would wear if he were home alone? I don't think that it would be cut-off shorts and a T-shirt. So from now on dress up in at least a polo shirt with presentable pants. Better still, a long sleeve dress shirt with some dress pants. And if someone asks, "What are you all dressed up for?" Just answer, "Oh, I thought I might go out later."

You should dress up even when you are home alone. This simple act will keep you in the Bond lifestyle mood more than anything else and keep you committed to your new purpose. And besides, you never know when you might have a visitor or when M might call you for a mission. So now you won't need the 'excuse the mess' line, nor have to tell them to wait while you change.

And while we're at it, throw out the T-shirt that says "Old Fart" and the one with the arrow pointing to the right with the words, "I'm with stupid." Because you may be old, but you're not a fart and you won't be hanging around with stupid people anymore, either.

Bond Is 'Heeled' and He Is Also 'Well Heeled'

If Bond is 'heeled' it means that he is carrying a gun. If he is 'well heeled' it means that he is prosperous. As in, the heels of his shoes are good so he must have money. Women are always checking out men's shoes to not only to see if he has money, but also to determine just what his attitude about personal appearance is.

Actor George Hamilton says, "If I see a guy with an expensive watch and bad shoes I've got him nailed." Don't let George Hamilton nail you. Keep your shoes in good repair and shined and don't forget the heels.

"If a good soldier dies with his boots on,
rest assured they are shined."
Jack Lemmon to Tony Curtis in ***The Great Race*****.**

Walk Like Bond

Now that you're walking in some nice looking shoes let's talk about walking. You know about fight director and stunt man Bob Simmons, right? He worked on most of the early Bond films. That's him at the beginning of *Dr. No* walking in the gun barrel of the trademark opening. Well, in his autobiography he said that he and Sean Connery decided together that Bond should not walk heavy footed as say John Wayne or Yul Brynner. Bond should walk 'cat-like' and gracefully. This indeed shows a certain kind of muscle tone and control.

I am also reminded of Diane Carroll's words when she first saw Sidney Poitier. "He moved like a graceful jungle cat." I take this to also mean energy under control. You'll find that, even though we can't change our natural walks so much, that if we tighten our stomach muscles and control our heel and toe movement with a little tighter energy, our gait smoothes out a bit. We don't want to do something that is unnatural to us. But if this gets us away from a heavy-footed bent over 'world on our shoulders' type of walk, then so much the better. So try not to plod along elephant style through the mall. Think of Bond and that cat-like walk. Careful though, don't overdo it, just smooth it out a little.

"Clothes Make The Man" or "Dress For Success"

There is truth in both of these slogans. What you wear is pretty much your own affair, depending on your personal tastes, your area's climate and the people that you hang out with. But you should take time to assess what you're wearing and where you want your clothes to take you.

When you do upgrade, it might take you a few days to get used to the new threads. But pretty soon you will. Be sure, however, that you don't go so overboard so that the clothes are wearing you, instead of you wearing the clothes. Also keep in mind the standard time, place and occasion when choosing what to wear.

Be careful not to fall into the conditioning left over from childhood of 'good clothes' and 'play clothes'. All your clothes should now be good clothes. Start paying attention to materials, their feel, comfort and fit. A cashmere sweater has a much different feel that a wool one, for example. And remember that it's better to have fewer good clothes, than hordes of marginal clothes. For your pocket book, good clothes last longer.

Get a trusted friend, preferably a woman, to help you pick out some upgraded clothes. But never wear anything that you are not comfortable in, or that you know you will never get used to no matter how long you wear them. Keep to the standard styles, because they will usually stay in style.

These are just a few suggestions. But the main thing to take away from this section is to upgrade your clothes so that you will remember to upgrade your life. Wearing better clothes is always a reminder that you promised yourself to continually advance toward your goals.

When Leaving For The Field

So you're going out of town. Maybe with a new girl. Don't forget whether you stay in two rooms or one, she's going to see your luggage. So get a couple of presentable bags before you take that important trip. Save the zipper bag for the gym.

Now that the subject of 'the field' has come up and you're about to put your new luggage into the trunk of you car, let's go to 'Q Branch' and talk about your equipment as well as your Bond car.

6

Q BRANCH

In Memory of Desmond Llewelyn 1914 -1999

"There can be forever many Bonds, but only one Q. I've lost a great friend. He went the way he would have liked, sitting at the controls."—**Pierce Brosnan December 20, 1999**

Creating vs. Competing

Before we start talking about all those gadgets and what they can do for us, let's talk about 'Q' and his staff. Did you ever wonder how they came up with such unique ideas? I know one thing; they didn't do it by competing with each other.

As mentioned earlier, any time you compete with someone you are remaining on his or her level. You are linked to their line of thinking. In order to be truly productive, successful and prosperous, you must switch from the competitive mind to the creative mind. Using your own individuality to express yourself creatively via your occupation. To come up with original ideas or new slants on old ones. This cannot be accomplished if you have a constant eye on your friends or co-workers.

Create; don't compete. Use your imagination to the fullest to move forward in your business, designing your own life. Remember if you try to keep up with the Joneses, they may be heading in the wrong direction. So imagine your way to success. That's why at The Walt Disney Studios, the animators and designers are called 'imagineers' and not 'competitors'.

Gadgets and More Gadgets

"Take this 007."
"Now?"
Thunderball

With so much wonderful and tempting electronic equipment on the market now, it's difficult to figure out exactly what we need. From which company? Which model? We don't want to get something merely as a toy, unless it fulfills that function (like a flight simulator program to unwind with). And we don't want to waste our financial energy on something we won't need after we've spent time and energy figuring out how to operate it.

All of us have our individual needs, tastes and interests. So one man's communicator can be another's prison. Example:

I knew an out of work actor in his thirties who started dating a successful woman. He moved in with her and she soon suspected that he did it strictly for free room and board, as he was a long time between acting jobs. She suspected that he was out playing around too much, either with his friends or possibly with other women. So she demanded he wear a pager and that he respond to her pages quickly, so as to check what he was doing. Yes, just like

Robert De Niro did to Sharon Stone in the movie *Casino*.This actor acquaintance became a prisoner just like Sharon, carrying his ball and chain everywhere he went. (Oh yes, you guessed it.The relationship quickly ended.)

On the other hand, I have a voice mail pager so that the right people can find me quickly and others can leave a message. It's the greatest tool for me. I've used it for seven years. Except for film shoots, I have no need for a cellular phone. I still prefer the methodology that I set up for myself early on. However, I'm ready to change should the need arrive.

That's why for this section I don't have an exact recommendation for a particular communication system. Except for you to think about your needs for now and acquire the appropriate electronic backup.

An important consideration is that once you decide on a pager, voice mail, or cellular phone, the next thing is to decide who gets what number for what device. You have to prioritize your electronics for your loved ones, friends, acquaintances, business associates and so on. So just don't be giving out your various numbers helter skelter.

The Home Computer And Email

To be brief, if you don't have a home computer, get one as soon as possible. However, if you don't want to put your financial energy there for now, then a least get a free email address that you can access via a hourly computer rental shop such as Kinko's or your library. This is no longer the communication gadget of the future, it is of the present. Just as web sites are now the business cards of the present.

Email allows you to communicate freely and quickly in your circle of influence. By using the internet, you can gather all the information you need to plan your missions in a few seconds. When I say missions, I mean everything from trips to choosing a university.

In under an hour a friend can teach basic email and internet functions to you. Other functions you can learn as you go. This will be an invaluable tool for your base of operations.

"It will engage and enfire the passenger ejector seat".
Q to Bond in *Goldfinger*

Today's mid-priced car is so technologically advanced compared to Bond's 1965 Aston Martin that in many ways it is superior to it. Remember that when you're driving around in your Ford or Pontiac.

The most important thing about your car is that it should be clean. Inside and out. Pay particular attention to the windows. Clean windows make the whole car seem cleaner. With the reverse true as well. You might have heard it said, "It's funny, but I think my car runs better when it's clean." That's because it's a well recognized illusion. This cleanliness is important for your mind programming. It is even more important for the impression it will make on the people riding in it.

"Why should I have a full tank?
All my friends live a gallon away."
—Jack Benny

That old joke of Benny's, as he acts the cheapskate, may bring a smile to your lips. But not to the lips of your date that's smelling the gas fumes in the station while you're filling up your car and holding up the fun. And will she smell the gas on your hands when you get back in the car? And will she think that she didn't even rate a fill up as part of your preparation for the date with her?

Once working with a guy on a film for a couple of months I noticed this first hand. At first, I didn't think much about it until others mentioned it, too. The guy was so cheap that he barely drove his own car, but when he did volunteer to drive you always ended up at the gas station before going on the appointed errand. At first I thought that he was just cheap, holding on to his gas money until he actually needed it. Then I realized that he didn't like being alone so he always waited for someone to accompany him to the station. At any rate this wasted everyone's time.

This particular guy was so interesting in his cheapness and anti-Bondness that when developing the James Bond lifestyle, I realized that many techniques were just the opposite of him. If you want to be Bond, I thought, just watch him and do the exact opposite. About eight or nine important ideas in this course are due to seeing the trouble he caused himself and others and then making a mental note to be sure to do the opposite. Which goes to show you that no one is completely useless. They can always serve as a bad example.

So keep that gas tank full, full, full, so that you're ready to go on that mission or pick up your Bond girl on a moment's notice. And then still have enough gas to get home.

"Let Hertz Put You In The Driver's Seat"

"I've just met the hottest new girl in town and she wants to go out with me. But I can't take her out in my old beat up jalopy. What am I going to do?"

"Rent."

Mentally back yourself up with rental car companies.

When you need a special car for large groups or that special date, rent one. Of course, you won't pretend that you own it to impress anyone. That's not necessary anyway. Just the fact that you're driving it is enough. The fact that your date or group can enjoy the comfort of it is enough. I myself, living in Tokyo, don't need or want a car here. However, when I'm in America, I drive a Lincoln. I don't own one, but I drive one.

If you rent cars frequently, especially when you fly into another town, you should examine one of the rental car memberships. Hertz Gold Card Club, for example, is $50 a year (they give you some discount coupons that you can use as a way of paying you back). They enter all your pertinent information into their computer, such as drivers license number, credit card numbers, address and so on. They give you a special number. Yeah, just like Bond. They also give you the special Hertz Gold phone number so that you just call in anytime that you want a car and make your reservation. They can even get you a car with only two hours notice. And the best part is that there is no more waiting in line or filling out the papers every time you need a car.

When you fly into another town, the comfortable Hertz bus picks you up at the airport. You get off at the Gold Club building before the non-members (who have to go to another building). You see your name in gold lights with a parking space number next to it and then you go to that space where your name is in gold lights above it. The trunk is open and waiting. You put in your luggage, drive to the check out gate, show your drivers license to the guard and you're off onto the streets. Now that's real Bond living. You'll be impressed with the convenience and so will anyone that's with you.

Returning the car, thanks to the new hand held computers, is even faster. You're checked in by an attendant, who is there to meet you and who prints out your final receipt before you even have time to get out of the car. Then you take your luggage to the nearby Hertz bus and in five minutes you're heading to your airline.

I recommend Hertz because they are constantly adding pickup and drop off points making them super convenient wherever you happen to be. But you can check out the others and compare. The Hertz web site is www.hertz.com.

"Bond liked fast cars and he liked driving them."
—Ian Fleming

Fast or slow, nothing ruins a trip or mission quicker than the unexpected accident. And aren't they all? You've heard many times about defensive driving and to "watch out for the other guy". Well, I've got a better mindset for you. There is no other guy. That's right. Inside all of those cars are no guys who "should have seen me coming." No driver that "should have given me the right of way." No one who "cut right in front of me."

What I mean by this is that you will now treat all cars just as if they are part of an arcade car race game. There are no drivers in those computer image cars, either. Just cars to get out of the way of. Objects to avoid and survive the drive. Cars that don't see you coming. Cars that don't know that they cut in front of you. You can't get angry at driverless cars.

So once you get out on the freeway, just avoid all those computer game cars. The way you do that depends on your speed and distance from the car in front of you. And also the distance that the car behind you is from you. If that driverless car is tailgating you, you should safely change lanes and let it go by. Let 'it' not 'him' go by. So checking the rear view mirror periodically will be part of your driving technique from now on, if it isn't already.

So to repeat, keep an extremely long distance between you and the car ahead. This will give you plenty of reaction time to assess an upcoming problem, decide your course of action and evade a car or bone crunching accident.

These days statistically speaking, you have a bigger chance of being hit by a cell phone-talking driver than a drunk. And that's not eliminating the drunks causing accidents, too. That's only making the drunks number two. So watch your speed, your distance from the car in front of you and avoid those computer game cars.

The Aston Martin Tracking Device

The tracking system in Bond's car was pretty cool in '65 and we thought that we'd never have anything like that in one of our cars. Well, now you can go one better and track your own car. The satellite navigation systems really do the job when you're out of town and would rather enjoy the scenery than struggle with directions and checking your map. They even have a woman's voice that tells you when to turn. You could almost do it blindfolded. One in a while the system goes down when you're between satellite cells. But all in all, this totally Bond gadget is really useful.

But before you invest your money in it, test it out in a rental car. Just request it when you make your next car reservation. However, be sure not to program it for your destination while you're driving. You don't want programming the navigational system to be counted as the number three reason for causing accidents.

"My number's on the card."
Bond, handing Sylvia Trench his business card in *Dr. No*

A business card is one of the handiest, cheapest and most overlooked 'gadgets'. It's got the information needed to get in touch with you, either by phone, email, or both. Order some and have them handy. That way even when you're jumping off a bus and a new acquaintance asks, "How can I get hold of you?" You can just toss her a card. Your card doesn't have to be fancy, just legible.

A Web Site As A Business Card

You don't have to be a giant corporation to have a web site. A personal web site that makes a positive statement about yourself could be just the ticket to enhance your image. Check out what the people are doing at www.xanga.com. This is a writer's community of sorts, with creative people posting photos, drawings, trip and daily diaries, news events and more. Click around and see how they are expressing themselves. Get the feeling of what each site tells you in terms of design, colors and content.

If this kind of creative expression is for you, then it wouldn't hurt your image to design your own site once you get something positive to post there. This is the place where I do my 'weekly action newsletter.' The fun thing is that others in the Xanga Community can leave you messages and you can leave messages on their sites as well. Outsiders can access and search around, too. It's free and you'll learn a lot about what other people are doing creatively. However, be extremely careful about what information you put on that or any web site. You don't want the color of your underwear to be common knowledge.

Later, you might excel at writing, web design, or other

forms of communication. You might even write your own novel and get it self-published and sell it on an internet store like Amazon.com. It can all start with a web site.

Q Branch will always be putting out new types of technology. Carefully select the ones that will add to your lifestyle and efficiency of action. That's what Bond does.

7

BOND GIRLS

Well, congratulations! You turned to this chapter first. That means your male hormones are at a normal level. So go ahead and read this chapter first. That's probably the main reason you bought the book. And I guarantee you that important and never before written about information is in here. Information that women have assured me is true. Women have told me, "Paul, you have hit the nail right on the head with 'the ultimate secret of women.'" But we'll get to the secret soon enough. First, let's clarify a few terms.

What Is A Bond Girl?

It sounds like a simple task to define. Beautiful? Ursula Andress of *Dr. No* was often called the most beautiful woman in the world. But for Bond girls, beauty is not even half of what makes them charming and alluring. Beginning with Ursula, who braved Dr. No's dangerous Crab Key island to collect shells and sell them for a profit, Bond girls have been intelligent, resourceful, self reliant, articulate and usually professional businesswomen. To think of them or any women in terms of only physical beauty is to miss the best points of what Bond women have to offer.

Speaking of the first Bond girl: Ursula Andress, whose *Dr. No* bikini recently auctioned off for $60,000 without her in it I might add is a lot more than just beautiful on the outside. I once saw Ursula and another actor being interviewed on the Merv Griffin Show. The actor said what a great lady Ursula was because on a mutual friend's funeral day, Ursula was in the widow's kitchen washing dishes. Now there's a really beautiful woman.

Who Is Your Bond Girl?

She is either your girlfriend, wife, women that you're dating or will be dating. So use your own image for the upcoming information. Of course, these 'Bond girls' are women, but 'girl' is used here because that's how they have been referred to in the media. Also this information doesn't suggest any particular lifestyle except the one that you choose for yourself, married or single.

She Sees You Checking Her Out

You're at a restaurant, mall or casino and you see an interesting woman and achieve missile lock on her and then suddenly she turns and catches you looking. Your natural tendency will be to jerk your eyes away. This demonstrates shyness or that your thoughts might have been lascivious – and now you feel caught. Don't suddenly jerk your eyes or head away from her. Calmly move your glance away. If you have a little confidence, you can add a hint of a smile, meaning; I just happened to notice you and yes, I was looking. This will end up being less embarrassing for both of you and will improve your confidence. Then you'll come away with a more satisfying experience for your mind to store away, instead of programming your self-image as a peeping Tom.

"I know a little bit about women."
Bond to Tracy in *OHMSS*

A little bit is all you have to know to be successful at entertaining a woman. Especially if that "little bit" is the ultimate secret of women. This is a secret that is never written about in any of those psychology or relationship books, valuable as they may be.

The secret can be found in the Cyndi Lauper song, *Girls Just Want To Have Fun*. In fact, the title is the secret. That's right, girls just want to have fun. What about love? Respect? Security? Of course. And most guys will give them that. But what most guys forget, after a few dates, is that they want fun. They want to go to movies, the opera, restaurants, amusement parks, resort hotels, Las Vegas, shopping, sight seeing, picnics, rodeos, any new place – there's no end to the list. But you can bet last on the list is sitting home with a beer and pretzels, watching the 10th football game in a row.

Girls like to look forward to a planned upcoming adventure. They also like the sudden spur of the moment outing.

For both men and women there is a deep psychological program that tells them if they are feeling completely loved or not. There are four elements:

Words: They were often praised as a child, so they believe words equals love.

Touch: Often touched as a child, they are programmed that touching equals love.

Gifts: The same thing applies here so the person must receive gifts to feel one hundred percent love.

Being taken some place: This one happens to be a strong one for many women. Even the Cass Eliot song of the seventies spoke of this, "Take her someplace she hasn't been before."

Okay, so where does that leave you? Well, considering that the idea of being taken some place gives many women the feeling of being totally loved, this is an all-important act. But even with that idea aside everyone wants to have fun. And this goes especially for women. So this means that you must become the director of fun. And actually it's good news, because all you have to do is arrange the entertainment. You don't have to worry about being cool. If you take a date to a cool place, make sure she has a good time, ask her what her goals and dreams are, she'll have a cool time and think that you're cool.

"She loved it, Paul"

After hearing my audio book, *How to Live the James Bond Lifestyle,* my old college dormitory roommate Steve called me and said, "Hey, I remember you saying in the dormitory that girls really want to have fun."

"Did I?" I asked. "I don't remember that."

"I do. Very clearly." Steve confirmed.

When I thought about it a little more, I started remembering girls mentioning about having fun on a date with a guy or that he was no fun. I kept hearing the word "fun" more than "he's cute" or "he's sexy". I had heard "cute" and "sexy" about popular guys and rock stars, from girls in high school. But when it got to serious dating in college it seemed that "fun" was the word I heard and the thing that the girls seemed to crave.

And then I remembered a guy named Carl who lived in the room next to mine in the dormitory. He dropped by excitedly one day and said, "Paul, I've got a date tonight. Where should I take her?"

I was flattered that he asked me for advice, so I didn't ask him what made him think that I knew what to do in San Francisco more than him. And since my dates were few and far between I wasn't exactly the best person to ask. Yet, I was always the guy going out to the movies with the other guys or by myself so maybe he thought that I might know a good flick for him to take her to. Also with the few dates I did have, it made me take each one seriously and I did plan them out well.

"Okay," I said. "First take the trolley car down to Market and Powell and walk up Powell Street a block. There's a quaint old time theater they're showing *To Sir With Love* at seven PM. But don't see the second feature because variety is important. When you come out of the theater walk up a block and get an ice cream at 31 Flavors. Then catch the cable car and give her a fun ride to Fisherman's Wharf. Then go to the small restaurant on the main street corner and get some clam chowder and whatever else she wants. Then take the cable car and trolley back to the dorm."

"Thanks," he said, "I'd better write that down." He ran back to his room. I forgot all about it until the next day when he came in my room and said, "Paul, I did exactly what you told me and she loved it."

Now that I remember it, I learned this variety dating idea from the Elvis Presley movie *Viva Las Vegas*. On his first date with Ann Margaret in the movie, he dances with her at the university, then takes her skeet shooting, then to a cowboy movie town, then a helicopter tour over Hoover Dam.After that water skiing on Lake Mead and then dancing at a nightclub. All this in the same day and night.

I was impressed by this because in the small town where I grew up guys just took their dates cruising around the main drag *American Graffiti* style. It was not only boring; it was a waste of female companionship, I thought at the time So when I got my chance, it was always a well planned date with plenty of variety. I often heard that they had "a lot of fun". So that's when I started getting the idea of what girls wanted, fun.

But Will She Like Me For Myself?

The question being asked here is: If I take a girl to lots of fun and exciting places will she just like me because I take her to these places or will she like me for who I really am?

It's a valid question that will come to the mind of younger guys. And the answer is this: You want to go to those places and enjoy the entertainment too, don't you? And if you do, then part of the real you is a person who likes to have fun doing those things. So that is the real you. Now, if you are just going there to razzle-dazzle the girl in order to get her to like you, you're a phony and just trying to manipulate her by taking her someplace that you don't want to go to. But of course, that's not you. You're not a manipulator and you do like entertainment and exciting places, so that is part of the real you.

This brings me to an important side subject. We've all heard of guys who wine and dine women until they get them to marry them and then don't want to take them anywhere after marriage. This often happened with the World War II generation that expected the wife to stay home all the time. This was fine for those days, but some husbands took it to extreme and the wives, try as they did, could never get their husbands to take them out, nor were they allowed to go out on their own. To me, this is breach of contract and false advertising. Because the man is advertising to the woman "Look how much fun you'll have if you stick with me" and then reneges on the deal once he's got her signature on the marriage contract. Thank God the women of today are stronger and have an easier out than they did in the fifties and sixties. Yet it still happens today with some of the younger guys.

What does that have to do with you? Keep taking her out even after she marries you. Because, here is the real deal. All great loves end in tragedy. Just like Bond and Tracy. One partner gets old, one partner gets sick, one partner dies. So enjoy "the hour of splendor in the grass, glory in the flower."

Steve Allen and Jane's First Date

When Steve Allen asked Jane Meadows out on their first date in New York, the 'in' thing to do was to go to a Broadway play or a high-class restaurant. But Steve was more inventive than that. He found out that a special show was being presented at the planetarium and he took her there. After the show Steve said, "Other guys would have taken you to Broadway or Sardi's, but I took you to the moon."

So when you're thinking of something to do to entertain your girl, let Steve Allen's date to the moon inspire you.

True Horror Story Number One

These stories I heard first hand. A twenty-five year old nurse living in Tokyo told this first one to me. She had just met a young dentist at her hospital and talked with him for a few minutes and then he asked her to go on a date on the upcoming Sunday.

"Do you think that he's a possible boyfriend?" I asked her before she was to meet the guy at the park."

"Oh yes. I think so."

"Well, tell me how it turns out," I said. She said she would and then went on her way to meet her potential boyfriend. I saw her a week later and asked how it went on the date.

"After twenty minutes I hated him," she answered.

"What did he do to you? Hit you?"

"No. We started walking in the park and I asked him what his favorite food was and he said, 'Nothing'. Then I asked him what kind of music he liked and he said, 'Nothing special.' And then I asked him what his hobbies were and he said, 'I don't have any.' So then after a while I said, 'Well it was nice meeting you' and we went to the bus stop and our separate ways."

I retold that story to an American friend of mine living in Tokyo and added, "So if a girl asks you what kind of food you like, choose any food, like pizza and say 'I LOVE pizza. I have to eat pizza EVERY day.'"

He said, "If I say that, the girl will think I'm crazy."

I replied, "Yeah, she'll think you're crazy, but not boring."

That very night a new girl that he was planning to take to the movies called him up and invited him to her place to eat before the going out. "It will only be pizza," she warned on the phone.

The word "pizza" triggered the story that I had told him just hours earlier and he replied, "PIZZA! I LOVE pizza!"

On the other end of the line came her excited voice, "Oh really? Really? Great." He laughed when he told me that true story and said he would always listen to my advice.

True Horror Story Number Two

Another young Japanese woman met a man via an 'arranged meeting' where she was introduced by a 'go between' as is the old Japanese custom. Of course these days, the couple can make up their own minds if they want to get married or not. But these introductions have the air of marriage about them, as opposed to just a date. And couples do get to see a photo of the intended beforehand.

The woman was interested in the man when she first met him at a restaurant with the go between. It was a great positive co-incidence that they both studied the teaching of an Indian guru named Sai Baba. This was destiny, she thought. "With this man I would probably give birth to a special spiritual baby," she told me.

On the next date she met him at a train station and said, "Hi, what do you want to do today?"

"I don't know," he answered. "What do you want to do?"

"Well, we can go to a coffee shop, I guess," she shrugged.

"Ok."

The next weekend they met at the same train station. "Hi, what do you want to do?" she asked.

"I don't know," he replied. "What do you want to do?"

"Let's go to a coffee shop, I guess."

"Ok."

And the next weekend. "Hi, what do you want to do today?" she inquired.

"I don't know. What do you want to do?"

After three coffee shop dates she figured that he was too boring to have a special spiritual baby with, especially if the conception would probably have to take place in a coffee shop.

But seriously, if the guy didn't have the imagination

or the interest to take her to a movie, a play, Tokyo Disneyland, Tokyo Tower, or a thousand other places that a big city has to offer, then her married life would end up being the same. He didn't know that "girls just want to have fun. Yeah, girls just wanna have fun."

A Kind Of Funny Horror Story for Number Three

An American buddy of mine related a story of a date he went on when he was twenty. It was a first date with a cute, petite, shy and very polite girl that he knew casually from high school. He took her to the 'in' movie at the time, the romantic *A Man and a Woman*.

He had enough gas in the car to get to and from San Francisco, about an hour drive each way from their town. They started out on a Sunday afternoon. He had enough money for the movie tickets. And that was all the money he had. Thank God, parking was free and the Bay Bridge toll was only a quarter.

When the movie ended he was worried that if he took her home early on this Sunday afternoon date it would be an insult to her and since he had no money for dinner he asked, "Did you like the movie?"

"Oh yes. Very much," she replied.

"Shall we see it again?"

"Ah … okay."

So they watched the movie again. When it was over it had been at least six hours since the girl had eaten and my buddy didn't even have popcorn money. And with her being very polite, she didn't bring up the subject of dinner or even a snack. So then they drove home which took another hour. At the door she politely thanked him for the date and went inside. "She probably dashed to the refrigerator," he laughed, embarrassed, remembering that date.

"I'm sure she did," I agreed.

The moral of the story is: Be sure to bring enough cash to feed your date. Some girls get darn right irritable if you don't at least give them popcorn.

These stories have the ring of sitcom humor to them. But ask yourself, do you want to be dropped by a girl you're interested in for being boring or broke?

Joe DiMaggio and Marilyn Monroe

Baseball great Joe DiMaggio was on his knees crying to his friend about Marilyn divorcing him after only ten months of marriage.

"Why did Marilyn divorce me?" Joe cried. "Is there another man?"

"How could I tell him," the friend said years later to Joe's biographer, "that she wanted to leave one of America's greatest sports heroes, because he was boring? How could I tell a man his ex-wife became his ex because she found him dull?"

Shakira Cain and Mira Sorvino

When asked why she liked her husband after twenty years of marriage, Michael Caine's wife Shakira answered, "Because he always wants to go someplace and do something."

When academy award winner Mira Sorvino was asked why she liked director Quentin Tarantino, she replied, "Because he's so much fun."

Well, have I convinced you with all these examples? Don't forget the ultimate secret, Mr. Director of Fun!

"You spent that much money on her?"

You know what the next line is, don't you? "... And you didn't get anything out of it?"

"Sure I did." I answered. "I had a nice dinner with a charming woman and then saw Frank Sinatra's concert with her. That's what I wanted to do. Who should I have taken ... you?"

That conversation actually took place between me and a guy I knew, whom later I found out was just as much of a tight wad with others as he was with himself.

So when some jealous cheapo says, "You spent that much money on her and nothing happened?" You can answer, "A lot happened. I had a great time and I've never spent money on a girl. I've only spent money on myself, having a good time with a girl."

"And if I have enough good times..."

Remember the movie, *Marty* starring Earnest Borgnine? He meets a not so cute girl and all his single friends with no girlfriends call her "a dog." His mother who's afraid of being left alone says, "She's not very pretty." His brother-in-law, who's having marital problems, tells Marty "Never get married." So Marty is under all kinds of pressure not to ask the girl out on a second date.At the end of the movie the guys are hanging around a coffee shop repeating their favorite question, "So what do you want to do tonight, Marty?" Marty finally goes to the pay phone and starts dialing. He says to his single friends, "All I know is that I had a good time with that girl and if I have enough good times with her I'm going to get down on my knees and beg her to marry me."

I gave you the two examples above for a reason. I'm not telling you to spend a lot of money on a date, or that you should get married. But I do want to warn you about people who have hidden agendas or issues about who you should date and how much money you should "spend on her."

My name is Bond. James Bond. Can we go dutch?

Who pays on a date? You do. If the girl insists on contributing to the restaurant bill and pulls out her money. Gently say, "That's okay. It's taken care of." If she pushes, then accept it as a gift, without making a scene out in public. But you should have the bill taken care of for whatever the entertainment is without the girl knowing about it. As in: Excusing yourself from the restaurant table and paying the bill secretly. So later when she asks, "What about the bill?" You can say, "It's taken care of."

And here's the big thing, as mentioned earlier; you will never 'spend money on a girl.' Because you'll only spend money on yourself. You wanted to take that girl out. You deemed her worthy of your time and cash. And you will, ninety percent of the time, take her to events that you wanted to go to in the first place. And if there is an event that she wants to go to that you're not interested in, you'll like to take her there just to make her happy, if it's someone you care about. And if the event is more expensive or boring than the girl is important to you, then you can politely say, "I'm sorry. That's not my kind of event. And with my schedule it would be difficult to go to at this time."

So, to repeat, the next time you hear a guy tell you, "You spent that much money on her and nothing happened?" You can honestly answer, "I've never spent money on a girl. I only spend money on myself."

Come to think of it, years have past since that Sinatra

concert, which I think about every time I hear one of Frank's songs and I'm still getting great value from the memory of that date. It was a rare opportunity to see Sinatra, but I was between film jobs so I had to use my credit card. And then I got another job and paid off the debt. Still seems like a good deal to me. And wow! Sinatra sang *The Lady is a Tramp* even better than in the movie *Pal Joey*.

So when your cheap friend says, "You took her to Las Vegas, paid for two rooms and nothing happened?" Just remember that you had the fun and your cheap friend didn't. And you know the more great times you have enjoying your James Bond lifestyle; the less time you're going to have for your cheap friend.

It Takes A Special Person

The James Bond lifestyle is not about throwing money around to look cool. On the contrary, you'll have to get value from every hundred-dollar bill you carry. But yes, I think you'll end up paying out an extra thirty percent over what you would pay if you didn't live this lifestyle.

You'll have to pay out a little more because of never going dutch, tipping properly, picking up the dinner tab or paying more than your fair share with your important friends, upgrading your apartment and clothes, taking more trips, buying more books, etc.

When you see yourself spending this extra money you'll have to remind yourself of what Charles Bronson said in *The Mechanic*, "It takes a special person to pick up the tab for that kind of living."

And you'll have to become a special person to do it. Yes, you'll be paying out an extra thirty percent, but you will start becoming more valuable in the market place to eventually earn an extra fifty percent over what you're presently making. You can deposit the twenty percent difference in your Bond account.

Don't forget the words, "This dream is for you so pay the price." The price will be money, study, working with your personality and just hard work in general. But it will be fun, hard work. When you get to where you want to be and you're hoping to surpass even that level of lifestyle, you'll say to yourself "What price?"

To paraphrase an old saying, "If you want more, you have to become more." Another one is, "It's more about what you become on your road to your dream than getting the dream." But I want to add that the dream is also unbelievably better that you can imagine, once you get it. So become that special person and pick up the tab for what you want. Make Charles Bronson and James Bond proud of you.

Gifts To Your Bond Girl

Gift giving is a special art. Meaningful gifts are those that speak to the person's special interests or hobbies. A book on a subject the person is interested in has more power than a gift with no personal connection. How about a page a day calendar with her favorite subject as the theme? Every day when she goes to the next page she'll think of you! Now that's getting value for your advertising dollar.

Though gift giving is important and comes under the law of circulation, you have to be a little careful when you meet that new girl and you're head over heels. There's something inherent in a guy's personal make up that, when he gets excited about a new girl, he wants to buy her some jewelry so as to get something on her finger or neck that marks her as his girl. Hence the words to an Elvis Presley song, "Won't you wear my ring around your neck. To tell the world you're mine, by heck."

This is fine, but remember you don't have to spend big money to do it. There are fine gemstones such as amethyst, garnet and onyx that can make a beautiful ring or necklace for two or three hundred dollars. Thus saving your important money for entertainment dating. The memory of the dates will still be there long after the girl is gone with the ring you gave her.

I'm not trying to be sarcastic here. But relationships do end, rings and necklaces come and go, but the memories remain, intact and indestructible for you to pull out, insert into your mental DVD player and relive. This is not only important for enjoying the memory, but for learning about yourself through what happened with that relationship. For example, what if anything, would you do differently, if that same situation comes up again?

So find meaningful inexpensive gifts to give her and circulate your bigger money on experiences and entertainment.

The Place Bond Is, Is the Place To Be

That goes for you, too. Did you ever go out with a habitual complainer? They come in both genders, though it seems like the men are in greater abundance in this category. They enter a nice restaurant and say, "What a dive." And then, "What a bad table." And then, "What bad food." And so on. I know that you won't do that. You'll go one better. I'll explain how.

When the manager is showing Bond to his room in *OHMSS*, he looks around the room and says, "This will do. This will do me nicely."

Now doesn't that sound good? Like he's more than satisfied? Like he's in control? Like he's putting his stamp of approval on the place? When your Bond girl or business associate hears you casually say something like "This is a nice place." Or "Ah, a good table." Or "This is nice," when entering a restaurant, hotel lobby or room they'll immediately fall into that feeling. Don't exaggerate, just say it casually. Even if the place you are at is older or even low class, you can say positively, "This is just like in the old time movies". Or "This is right out of the wild west." Any positive casual statement will do. When in doubt, just copy Bond. "This will do. This will do us nicely."

Bond's Big Problem With Women

He keeps losing them in the field. They get lost, hurt, or worse. Note Tilly Masterson's departure due to Oddjob's steel rimed hat. So whether you're on a short date or on a trip with your Bond girl, watch out for her safety.

Now usually the big bad things don't happen and they won't to you and your girl. It's the little things that get you. Like falling down in the shower, fingers and toes crunched in a car door, falling down stairs, tripping over any number of things. Or the biggest danger, crossing the street. In San Francisco, for example, two pedestrians a day are hit by cars.

Particular attention should be paid to your driving when you're on a date. A charming woman sitting next to you can break your concentration. More than one accident has occurred by an osculation that couldn't wait until the destination.

So watch out for your precious cargo and bring her back safely from the field.

"Well, I guess I won't need these."
Bond says as he pushes away the oysters when the girl tells him they'll sleep in separate beds.

I didn't get it the first time I saw that scene in *You Only Live Twice*. But it was later explained to me that oysters are thought to contribute to a man's virility. Now it's been proven scientifically that oysters contain zinc and men need zinc for virility. (fifteen to thirty mgs a day.)

But that's not what this section is about. It's about being virile and then the girl tells you to sleep in your own room. You did invite her on this trip with the promise of two rooms. Of course, you hoped for the same thing Bond was hoping for. But she's just not ready for you. She came on the trip with the intention to look at the scenery and not the ceiling. Perhaps you're just not her type, or maybe next time. What to do?

Nothing. Oh, you can repeat Bond's oyster line to yourself, if that will lighten up your natural disappointment. Or go down to the hotel gym and work out or swim laps in the pool. But that's all you'll do, except be careful. Disappointment intensified becomes anger. And you don't want her to see your disappointment, let alone your anger.

The thing is this. If you stay cool, stay James Bond cool and don't get weird on her, she will learn to trust you. Trust you to always be fun without being pushy. In that, there's a chance for another time, even possibly tomorrow night, or on another trip, or when you get back. But guys that get weird on girls, that become pushy or angry, are seldom given a second chance. And never a third.

George Hamilton sums up this idea perfectly. "I've never forced the issue of sexual involment. Women make that decision. And as long as you make them feel comfortable, you'll arrive there quicker than guys breathing down their neck."

A Well Edited Date

A well-planned date should flow smoothly and have a good ending, just like a good movie. Plan where you'll park, for example. On a date use the convenient paid parking that is next to your destination, such as a movie theater or restaurant. (VIP valet parking if they have it.) Save the far away free parking for when you're alone or with your buddies. Later, as you move up in prosperity you'll always use the most convenient parking because your time will be more valuable than the parking fee.

The thing that you should pay the most attention to, for a well-paced date, is the ending. You've been out with your friends where there is always one guy who says, "One more nightclub," or, "One more game of pool. One more ride on the roller coaster." They "one more" for so long that you end up dragging yourself into your apartment at one AM, tired and with no time to prepare for tomorrow. Remember those experiments? Not so good. Right?

So let's say that you take a girl out for dinner and a movie and then when you come out of the theater you can feel that this is the high point and there's not really enough energy or feeling to do something else. That's when you should end the date and take her safely home. Sure you want to spend more time with her, that's why you asked her out. But if it's a new date especially, end it on a high note. Don't let the evening grind down to a slow drag and then boring conclusion, before deciding to end it.

Of course, if you two are really hitting it off and you can feel the energy, then you can proceed to another attraction. However, be aware of the energy and flow of the day or evening and be prepared to call it a night, for the sake of a good ending and perfect date.

Now this is where good planning is of the utmost

importance. If you have the entertainment planned, then you can move on to it. But if there is nothing planned, don't try to extend the date just for the sake of more time, or 'the longer the better'. Remember she has things to do at her home, especially if it's a work or school night. And always resist the temptation to say, "How about one more ... ?"

"Do you think she's worth going after?"
"I wouldn't put it that way, Sir."
M and Bond in *Thunderball*

How do you know if this new girl might be the right one for you? Here is a key: If the more you find out about her, the more you like her, then you're heading in the right direction. But if, the more you find out about her the less you like her, then maybe you should consider dating others.

What Am I Doing Here With Her?

Suppose you're on a first date with a girl at a restaurant and then start thinking, "She doesn't have this quality. She doesn't have that quality. What I'm I doing here with her, anyway?" Then your disappointment makes you clam up and you hurry through the evening so you can get rid of her.

Well, of course, this is the wrong mindset. What you should be doing is acting like she is the one for you; not to the point of you running off and getting married, but to the point of being open and friendly in your communication and entertaining. You probably won't date her again, but she's a spiritual being going through a human evolution on this planet just like you. So why not find out about her? Why not practice your communication skills? Why not find out about her dreams and pass on some of the techniques that you're learning in this book?

So if she's not the one, get into the feeling that she is. It's good programming for your mind, in that if you enjoyed the evening like she is the one, you're programming your subconscious that you're on the right road to finding the girl of your dreams.

"I don't want to be going with you."
John Travolta as Tony Manero in *Saturday Night Fever*

John Travolta makes a good point here. The first girl that he starts practicing for the disco contest with really loves him. She says, "Let's 'make it', Tony."

"Nah, if we're dancing together and 'making it', it would be like we're going together. And I don't want to be going with you."

Well, Tony's got an interesting philosophy. He thinks sleeping with a girl doesn't make her his girlfriend, nor does dancing with her. But doing both makes her his girlfriend.

This brings to mind an acquaintance that kept saying that the girl he was taking to dinner, going on trips with a nd sleeping with wasn't his girlfriend. "She's not my girlfriend, honest." he would repeat. Well, Travolta in that movie would have given him an argument. He would say, "If you're going to dinner with her, going on trips with her and sleeping with her, then Buddy, she's your girlfriend."

You'll know she's your girlfriend when it comes time to break up with her or you find yourself pressured into marrying her because a couple of years have gone by and now she has squatter's rights.

I've seen this happen a couple of times and heard and read about it many times. A guy gets a 'convenient' girlfriend while waiting for his 'true love' and suddenly she starts hitting him over the head with a preacher. Now this is no joke when it happens to you. But whether you decide to take the responsibility for an 'in between girlfriend' while you're waiting for 'the one' or go it alone until she appears, is up to you. Just remember the words of Tony Manero, "If you're going out with her and sleeping with her, she's you're girlfriend no matter what you say or think."

You Can't Change Her

And she can't change you. We are all in a state of growth and we grow at our own speed. Sure you can encourage, but don't think that you can change a person. When someone wants to change you, what do you do? You resist, don't you?

So never interfere with someone's free will, especially when it comes to things like drinking, drugs and smoking. Those things are highly addictive and take special commitment and even professional counseling to stop. So when you say to yourself, "If only she would stop smoking ..." Well, you can think it, but don't tell her. If tobacco smoke gives you a headache, then even if she looks and acts better than your favorite Bond film girl, it's not going to work. Having a constant headache on a honeymoon trip will only be the start of your problems. So it's time to look elsewhere.

I once went on a date with a beautiful and charming woman named Karen. We were both age thirty. She was perfect for me and I think she liked me, too. But her smoking at dinner, which I never mentioned, gave me a headache. She lived in Los Angeles, I lived in San Francisco, so I let the distance do the job of not moving forward with her. I just stayed in touch by phone and met her a couple of times for dinner (and a headache) to remain friends. She was dead of lung cancer by age forty-one. I miss her friendship still.

When You Want An In Depth Relationship

There comes a time in every relationship where one of the partners wants to move forward to the next level. These levels go from dating, to friends, to lovers, to commitment and possibly to marriage. Problems come when the couple doesn't agree on moving to the next level.

If you are the one that wants to move the relationship up to the next level, what should you do? Well, at some point you'll have to say to the girl that you want an in depth relationship. She will either want it or not. If she doesn't want it, then no matter how good she looks to you physically or personality wise, cross her off your list of potential lovers. Is this being cold? Someone might say that you're being very cold. But real coldness is what you're going to get if you don't respect the girl's wishes and try to push, beg, or manipulate her to the next level. Once again, never encroach on someone's free will.

You will feel rejected and disappointed, but here is where your mental and emotional toughness can come into play and rescue you. At this time, it might help if you tell yourself, "Be a lover, don't need a lover."

You won't want to hear this next expression. I sure didn't. But when a relationship ends or won't intensify all you can do is "Get ready for the next one."

If you keep at it you will eventually find the kind of relationship that Bond had with Tracy in *OHMSS*.

"What if when I meet her in the flesh,
I don't come up to expectation?"
"Just see that you do."
Bond and M in *Thunderball*

Don't come up to her expectations, surpass them. How? Use your personality to express your true individuality. Have confidence that your higher self will guide you throughout the relationship. Have fun giving and don't worry about the receiving part. That part will take care of itself. And finally relax and enjoy the whole process. And if the two of you are mismatched, but you still want to go along for the adventure, then enjoy it for what it is.

I'm not suggesting that you stay in a mismatched relationship just for the adventure, but sometimes you get stuck, addicted and in love where you can't get away, even if you want to. So once in a while step back from the vertigo of this thrilling adventure with this woman that is not right for you and say, "Wow! Just like in a Bond movie."

But always try to remember that because of the mismatching, it will probably end and end soon. So get ready for the big fall, like James Stewart in *Vertigo*. But I guess he thought that Kim Novack was worth it while it lasted.

Richard Gere - Priscilla Presley - Mike Tyson

Groucho Marx said, "I always date two girls at a time because I hate to see a girl walk home alone." As a joke that's funny. As a real life happening, it landed Mike Tyson in prison.

Date rape had occurred, but the girl waited two days before reporting Tyson to the police. What happened? When Tyson forcefully 'finished' with the beauty pageant contestant in his hotel room, he told her to go downstairs and his limo driver would take her home. He didn't even take her downstairs, let alone take her home himself. And then he never called her. The girl felt humiliated and finally after two days with no call from Tyson, reported the rape.

This is a serious crime. Yes, it was proven that the girl was raped. But it is also believed in the Tyson camp that if he would have taken her home and taken her out the next day, or had at least called her, she would have not reported it. (Not that she shouldn't have.) Again this is a very serious crime. However, it can teach us a lesson. But first another example.

Priscilla Presley went on a date with Richard Gere and stayed overnight at his house, willingly and happily. She admitted having a good time, but a week later she "wanted to kill him." Why? Because he never called her.

What do these two stories teach us? I think these stories are screaming out that: When the girl stays overnight with you, especially the first night, you should take her home, invite her to brunch the next day, call her after that to see how she's doing and send her an email saying "Thinking of you". Not that she's going to press charges, as in the above serious crime, but so you at least treat her as a human that you've made intimate contact with.

So put in that extra energy; give her that extra attention no matter how busy your are at work the next day. Pick up the phone and dial. Don't leave the girl sitting there at home or work wondering what that time spent with you was all about. Wondering now that she has shared her most intimate self with you, if you're going to drop her? Was she just something that you used for the night? Do you even remember last night?

So pick up the phone the next day and talk to her for a few minutes. Invite her out again, even if you have decided for some reason that you don't want to spend too much time with her in the future. If that's the case then end it slowly, gently and politely after a while. You don't want to end up in someone's autobiography as an insensitive Clyde, like Richard Gere did.

Call Me When You Arrive Home

Yeah, just like your mother made you do when you got back to your college dorm room. Only you use this when your girl is driving home by herself. She'll love it when you say, "Be sure to call me the first thing when you get home, so that I'll know you got there safely."

Now if you really like her you'll naturally want her to do it. But let's say you're not so worried about that. You know she'll get home all right, so why should you have her bother you with her phone call? Hey, it's an easy thing for you to do. She gets home. She calls you. You turn down the sound on the TV and say, "Hi, are you home? Great! I had a nice time with you tonight. Pleasant dreams." Then hang up and turn the sound back on to *The Spy Who Loved Me* title sequence with Carly Simon singing, *Nobody Does It Better*.

Home By Taxi?

If she's going home by taxi, be sure to give her some small bills that she can use to easily pay the fare and the tip. But most importantly, look inside the cab and see the driver's taxi license and say, "Okay Fred Henderson (his name from the license) take her to 320 Belmont Street (her home)." Another way is to read the driver's license number and say "Hey your license number 38654 is the same as my phone number."

This way he'll know, and more importantly she'll know, that this cab driver will do everything in his power to drive her politely and safely home.

Giving To Her Is Not Enough

I actually saw this with my own eyes. A man in his thirties who was very cheap and selfish saw a woman that he liked and got a date with her. He lavished her with all kinds of gifts, special dates and attention. But after a month, the girl got sick of his attitude and general personality. So she stopped dating him.

You see he gave only to someone that he was interested in getting. He gave only in order to get something for himself. But it doesn't work that way, does it? He did not have the atmosphere of giving in his aura, personality, voice tone, body language or word choice. So the woman finally wised up and called it quits.

So when you give, it has to be to everyone in your circle. It has to be to kids and old ladies that you don't expect to get anything back from, except the fun of seeing them happy and taken care of.

You have to give of your time, feelings and energy with no expectation of return directly from those people. But when you do give it will accumulate in some kind of 'universal energy bank' and it will at various times of your life come back to you. It may come back as good luck, or health, or a business break, or a love relationship, or avoiding a near accident. Just know that it will come back. It certainly will come back in friendship and good will and give you an aura of giving that the right girl will recognize.

The Only Way To Get The Girl

In a way, this secret may be stronger than "girls just want to have fun." But if you use both of these techniques you'll create a powerful aura for attracting the girl of your dreams or re-energizing the one you have now. Like Pilar Wayne said,

"Working on *The Alamo*, I fell in love with John all over again." That was because John Wayne was 'in the flow' and doing his dream project that had taken him years to get off the ground. The Duke was in his element and he handled everything well, making him super attractive again. But that's only part of this secret.

To see the only way to get the girl rent the movie, *Ground Hog Day*, starring Bill Murray. This is the only movie that shows you how to get the girl. At first Murray secretly finds out information about the girl and then pretends that he has the same likes as her. His deceitful and insincere strategy doesn't work.

Finally he gives up and begins to use his time constructively. He learns the piano, ice carving and then more importantly begins helping people and befriending people (even the aforementioned old ladies). Now he has little time for the girl and she gets curious when everyone seems to know Murray and like him. She sees people thanking him for the various things he's done for them. She sees him give a surprise gift to some newlyweds and be the center of attention of everyone he's helped. Now Murray is just being himself and is 'in the flow', busy with his single productive life. So the girl becomes interested in him, instead of him chasing her.

Also coming into play here is the old adage from the *The Wizard of Oz*, "A heart is not judged by how much you love, but by how much you are loved by others." Maybe when we were children we didn't understand the full meaning of that line. If we think about it now, we can understand that when we've sincerely given unselfishly to people with love, then that love is returned, showing that our heart is good.

When Murray started improving himself he makes himself more interesting, fun and attractive. So watch this movie closely and get the feeling of it. Self-improvement and growth are very exciting things to watch. Just think how many exciting movies are based on the theme of self-help. The Rocky films certainly fall into that category.

So rent *Ground Hog Day* and see how to get the girl. You'll not only attract a Bond girl, but the right kind of Bond girl for you.

Shop Till She Drops

If you go shopping with her, be sure to understand that you are there for the duration. If she wants to go it alone for a while you can find a book store, video shop or an Orange Julius stand where you can sit it out. If it's a shopping mall with a movie theater, so much the better. Give her your cell phone or pager number and tell her to vibrate you when she's finished. This way you can enjoy a movie while she's hitting the stores.

If you go on the trek with her to carry her bags, good luck and try to keep an upbeat expression on your face. Once again your ex-girlfriend may see you with her and you don't want her to think your new girl is a drag. (You don't want the new one to think you're a drag, either.)

Her Luxury Restroom

"I have to go to the restroom." Well, now that you've got a Bond girl that you're dating, you'll be hearing those words a lot. Usually when you're stuck in traffic minutes after you left a restaurant that had a convenient restroom for her to use.

The thing to remember is, don't take her to a gas station

restroom. If you can, drop her off at a first class hotel where she can 'sandbox' in style in the lobby restroom. At least take her to a clean looking chain restaurant like McDonald's where you know the restroom will be half way decent. Best is to get her to a hotel lobby.

The Party Has To Stop

This is different than 'the date needs to have a good ending'. What this means is that, a guy takes a girl on a whirlwind adventure of resorts, airplanes, rental cars, restaurants, concerts and skiing and doesn't stop until his money, credit and job are gone. And then finally the girl is gone when the adventure has run down into poverty.

The girl can't be blamed. It was the guy who introduced himself as this non-stop action guy with limitless funds and fun. So when the guy becomes jobless, in debt and with no gas to drive the girl around, she stuck around for a few weeks and then she split the scene. A scene that he created because he didn't stop the party to get back to work.

There are many such stories. So balance and pace are needed for luxury dating. Remember: Balance includes a steady source of income and an eye on the spending budget.

Judge Dee And His Three Wives

A friend of mine had just started dated a beautiful and charming woman. But a month into it he complained to me that she was leaving him messages everyday on his answering machine and he didn't want to always be obliged to return her call. "I'm busy with work," he said. "I can't talk with her or leave her a message everyday."

"How long do your phone conversations with her last?" I asked him.

"Oh, about five minutes," he replied with an annoyed voice.

I then proceeded to tell him about this made for TV movie that I had once seen called *Judge Dee and the Monastery Murders*.

It's a period story in old China where this Chinese detective of sorts is investigating murders at a monastery. He has brought his three wives along with him and at one point when he and his assistant are hot on the case, two of his wives approach him. "Wife number three is sick," wife number one reports to him.

"Well, I'm busy," Dee says. "Attend her."

"She would really like to talk with you." Wife number two says.

"I'm in the middle of something very important," he says. "I don't have time right now."

"Oh, if you could just give her a minute of your time she would be so encouraged to get well," wife number one says.

"Oh, all right." Dee groans. "I'll talk to her."

When he enters wife number three's room, Dee's entire demeanor changes. "What's this I hear," he consoles as he approaches her bed. "They tell me that you've become ill. I was so shocked to hear this."

"Oh, I'm sorry." she says. "I just feel a little weak."

"Well, you've got to get better for me," he says with great and gentle concern in his voice as he holds her hand. "I can't work or concentrate knowing that you're sick. I'm so worried about you. Please get better, so as to ease my mind."

"Oh yes I will," she smiles gently. "I'll try very hard to get well right away."

"That's good. Please get well for me. Now I'll leave you

alone so that you can rest."

"Thank you for your kind words."

"Get well soon," he says as he leaves the room. He closes the door and then walks up briskly to his assistant. "Okay," Dee orders with determination, already forgetting his third wife. "Let's get back on the job."

After telling this story to my friend I said, "So you've got this beautiful new girl and you can't put on an act like Judge Dee for five minutes on your car phone while driving to work?" To his credit he got the point right away and from that time on enjoyed his phone talks with her and was no longer annoyed by her 'over-attention'.

We all have various people who want our attention. Different 'hats' to wear, so to speak. We have the son hat, the brother hat, the boyfriend hat, the employee hat and the friend hat. So when one of these people needs your attention, just change your hat like Judge Dee did from his detective hat to his husband hat and then back again to his detective hat.

Especially when it comes to your Bond girl, know how to put on your boyfriend hat and how to wear it well while you have it on.

If You Have Three Wives

If juggling girls is what you're doing now, or considering doing, here are a couple of horror stories for you. While we were working on a movie I made, two actresses told me the following stories.

Story #1:

"I had one boyfriend in New York that I loved and

one in Texas that I was using for money because he was rich. The New Yorker knew about the Texan. But the Texan thought I was being true to him. Well, one night I wrote a love letter to my New Yorker telling him that I really loved him and that I didn't even like the Texan and that I was just using him for money. Then I wrote to the Texan and told him I loved him. Unfortunately when I stuffed the envelopes after addressing them I accidentally put the wrong letters in the envelopes and mailed them. The Texan called me a couple of days later, yelled at me over the phone, and dropped me cold."

I can't remember what she said happened to the New Yorker, but if you're going to juggle two lovers you'd better pay attention to letters, email and whom you're talking to. But sometimes fate alone will come in and mess with you, as this next young woman will explain.

Story #2:

"I was sitting in my hotel room talking to my secret boyfriend who was a long time friend of my real boyfriend. I was going on and on about our secret trip to Mexico and how much I loved him. What I didn't know was that my real boyfriend had called the hotel during that secret call and the hotel operator inadvertently patched him into my line with me talking. He listened for about five minutes and then finally yelled, 'Janet, tell him to hang up.' I was paralyzed with shock and fear."

I don't remember the outcome of that story either. However, there's a lesson in there somewhere. I'll leave it to you to dig it out.

Breaking Up Is Hard To Do

"What I did was for King and country. You don't think that I got any pleasure out of it, did you?"
Bond to just bedded villainess in *Thunderball*

A great line indeed. And you'd be surprised how many guys use these kinds of put-downs when an argument or break-up occurs. It's just a pride thing, like in high school, where the guy says, "She didn't break up with me, I broke up with her."

Hey, what difference does it make? It didn't work out and that's sad, but be polite as you can when that happens. Even give a compliment or feeling of good will if you can, before you go home and drown your sorrows in the 'shaken not stirred' stuff. You can say something like, "I'm really sad that it didn't work out, but I had a great time with you while it lasted. And I will always think well of you and speak well of you."

Actually saying something polite like that will make her think that you aren't so broken up about it; a kind of reverse pride, or pride by compliment. It leaves the door open for her. This is important because they often come back. And that phone call out of the blue where her first words are, "Hi. Do you still like me?" will really make your day.

No Woman Hates Me

I think there is something to be learned or at least remembered from the movie *South Pacific*. When Mitzi Gaynor responds negatively to Razzano Brazzi's having married an island girl, he says this: "I make no apologies. I came to the island a young man and lived as I could. But I have not been ungenerous. No woman hates me or would want to harm me."

Knowing his personality she responds, "No woman could."

This speaks well for that character's personality and handling of his women. It's something to remember when breaking up. Try to do it so that she doesn't hate you or would want to harm you.

A Tip From The World's Greatest Playboy

Did you see the 1970 movie, *The Adventurers*, based on the Harold Robbins novel? The lead character, Dax Xenos, was based on a real European playboy named Porfirio Rubirosa, who married a couple of rich women and then had the money to party throughout the world. For a while Sammy Davis Jr. hung around with him and one day asked Rubirosa, "How do you do it? You attend every party, play polo, date women and go yachting, day in and day out. Yet, you always look great and you're never tired."

"What I do, Sammy, is pace myself. I never go to a party too early and I never stay too late. I only drink a little and I'm careful what I eat. And even if I'm entertaining a woman, I always get my sleep."

This is great advice for any active person. Being a film director, I've been associated with many actors, stuntmen, cameramen and the like. On a movie the professionals, the ones who want to have a long career always get their sleep every night. The amateurs, who are just giving movies a try, party all night with other amateur crewmembers. By the end of the first week the amateurs are zombies on the set, while the professionals are fresh, energetic, prepared daily and can go the eight-week production schedule with the same daily energy. Why? Because they pace themselves – they sleep.

When Clint Eastwood decided to direct his first movie, he asked veteran director Don Siegel (*Dirty Harry*) for some directing advice. Siegel said only this: "Get plenty of sleep."

Anybody can party or work day and night for a week using five cups of strong coffee a day to keep them going. But by the next week they are checking into a hospital, incapable of writing or even remembering their name to register. I've seen it.

So if you're really interested in living the James Bond lifestyle to the fullest, you will pace yourself in all things dealing with energy, including money and your body. The following old joke will clarify:

A young bull and an old bull are standing on the top of a hill looking over a herd of cows down below. The young bull says, "Let's run down the hill and 'get' us one of those cows."

The old bull replies slowly, "No. Let's walk down the hill and 'get' them all."

All Play and No Work Makes Bond a Dull Agent

I have often heard women say about a man they went on a first date with, "He's not my type." When I ask for clarification they say, "Oh, he just wants to relax and play and is not interesting in working or doing anything."

I immediately understand what they are saying. To be interesting, a man has to be productive. He has to have plans to accomplish something. I also believe that full time relaxing and playing becomes repetitive and boring. To relax for a couple of weeks after completing a goal is wonderful. But a working vacation is better still.

So I say, forget the lazy life, just hanging around to see what comes. Work hard and play hard in proper proportion.

Yes, girls want to have fun, but they also want to see their man creating, accomplishing and improving.

Tyrone Power Gives Gene Hackman Advice

I heard Gene Hackman tell this story: "I was at a friend's home when I was young and trying to break into acting. He was talking on the telephone and then he handed the phone to me and said, 'Here talk to Tyrone Power.' I was flustered when I took the phone, but I managed to ask Mr. Power if he had any advice for my acting career. Power said, 'Yes, it's important how you handle your women.' That was the only advice he gave me."

When I heard that story I was just starting out in my directing career and wondered how that advice could pertain to any career, let alone acting or directing. But later thinking it over and doing more studying of the careers of men, I could see that many men have been ruined by choosing the wrong woman and have been successful by choosing the right woman.

It usually turns out that the man who is driven by love and sex does great things. The man who is driven by sex alone, fouls up his business and his life.

The main thing to remember, I think, is Tyrone Power's general statement of, "It's important how you handle your women."

8

YOUR MISSION

All the information that you have been given up to now will be of little use if you don't have a mission. We are given so much mental, physical and emotional power that it would be a real waste not to use it. That's why goals and challenges are necessary to life. So that we can learn to use and control our great power.

America's founding fathers knew this when they wrote, "All men are created equal." They didn't say "born equal". They said "created equal". Because some of us are born rich or poor, with great parents or not, in a good location or not. But we are all born with the same mental and subconscious powers. We in America are lucky enough to be guaranteed the "pursuit of happiness." Note that we are not guaranteed happiness, only the pursuit of it. In that "pursuit," which has the idea of "taking action," lies your chosen mission.

Code Name: Operation Go For It

What mission is right for you? Anything that adds to your education, vitality, security or creative expression, as long as it doesn't take away from someone else or encroach on someone else's freedom. Whatever you're feeling that you want now is right for you. If a new job or residence is what you feel you need now, then that's what you should go after.

Of course, general lifestyle upgrade is of immediate importance to you now, because that's why you're putting your time and energy into this book. So write down the first mission you want for yourself. And give it an empowering code name like, 'Operation Thunder Apartment'.

Bond's Four Step Strategy

In *OHMSS*, Bond is searching for the villain Blofeld. How does he proceed with his mission? He asks. He asks the right person, the well-connected gangster named Draco, for information about Blofeld. Draco says if Bond will consider marrying his daughter, he'll give him the needed information. Bond makes a deal with Draco by hinting he'll continue dating his daughter. Draco tells Bond about another contact that may know of Blofeld's hideout. So Bond continues his mission by asking the next contact.

These four steps are basic and simple, but few people use this 007 strategy. Perhaps because of its simplicity. However, you will take the proper action when you have a mission. So when you want something:

1. Ask.

2. Ask the right person.

3. Be willing to give something and make a deal.

4. Continue asking other 'right' people.

This final step of continuing is the most powerful step in accomplishing any mission. Without it Bond would still be in Jamaica trying to decide to go to Crab Key Island or not.

Another word for this final step is 'Perseverance'.

The Shortest Speech In History

Winston Churchill was asked to give a speech to graduates at Oxford University. He sat on the stage while the university president gave him a five-minute introduction. Then Churchill stood, walked to the mike, gave a six-word speech and then sat down. The six words were, "Never, never, never, never give up."

The Great Strike Out King

When Babe Ruth held the record for the most home runs, he also held the record for the most strikeouts. What does this tell us? In order to hit a home run you have to swing the bat a lot. You have to not be afraid to strike out and walk back to the dug out with all those disappointed fans looking at you. After that strike out, you have to get your mind together to try for a home run again with your full mental and physical powers.

This story also tells us that success is a game of numbers where lots of action and risk taking gets results.

"But I'll be thirty-eight years old by then."

A young man I know once said, "I really want to get my college degree while I'm working. But if I go to night school, it will take me eight years. I'm thirty now, I'll be thirty-eight years old by then."

"How old will you be in eight years if you don't go to night school?" I asked him.

"Ah ... thirty-eight."

Don't let your age, or the age you will be when you finish your goal, deter you.

The Only Time You Lose

When is that? The answer is simple: When you give up.

Bond Never Gives Up

You've seen Bond beat up, outmaneuvered, outsmarted, outfought, betrayed and near death. But you've never see him give up. Without perseverance nothing can be accomplished. Perseverance is a stronger and more necessary quality than intelligence, talent or education. We have all seen intelligent, talented and educated people who are failures. Why? Because they gave up.

When you're climbing the mountain to your goal the conditions are always changing. When the sun is out and things are going well, that's the time to run up the mountain while you have the chance. It's not the time to rest. When the rains come, you'll feel like giving up. But don't do it. Just pitch a tent, keep your business sign hanging outside and wait for better weather.

I've seen so many people quit and walk away from their dreams, usually because of social and financial pressure. It's okay to take a break, but don't tear up your business cards or take down your shingle. You don't have to tell everyone that you've quit. Just get better and prepare for the next opportunity. In fact, success is when preparation meets opportunity.

I've often wondered why people have to make the big loud statement of "I quit!" or "I told my agent to go screw himself!" Or "I threw all my scripts in the garbage!" One day passing a novelty shop I found out the answer. I saw a comedy sign in the window. It was meant for laughs, but I saw the truth in it and then I understood why so many people give up and tell everybody loudly that they definitely quit their goal. The sign read: "It feels so good, now that I have given up all hope."

From what I've seen, the dangerous age for giving up is exactly 26. Why is that? The really strong people continue three or four years after college pursuing their dreams. But they start to run out of gas exactly four years later. It's always because the girlfriend, wife or even parents put the pressure on to "get sensible and get a regular job." Actor Bruce Dern had made 24 movies and his mother still told him, "Come back home and do something sensible."

Of course you should work to support yourself, but you still should also be available to take action on your goals when the opportunity presents itself.

Tom Cruise Gets Great Advice

Well, it was actually Tom Cruise's character in the movie *Risky Business* that gets the advice from his high school friend. "Sometimes you just have to say 'What the hell.' Saying 'What the hell' brings freedom. Freedom brings opportunity. And opportunity makes your life. So your parents are out of town for two weeks? You've got the car? You're home alone? What the hell."

Well, Tom gets into a lot of trouble by getting involved in too risky a business. But he does grow, gain confidence and gets a hot, if dubious, girlfriend.

So fellow Bond fans, you've got a goal? Got a plan? Got a few bucks saved? What the hell!

Your Fantasies Becoming Your Realities

Now pay attention to this one. This is of utmost importance. So slow down here and really take this in.

Everyone has fantasies about some unique experience that they want to have. When they tell you about it they really get into the emotion of it. And then they shrug it off thinking that it's not even worth their effort to try to get this fantasy, because it will never happen.

I've long since given up on encouraging people to go after their fantasies. The reason is that most people would rather have you give them your attention and energy concerning their fantasies, rather than investing their own attention and energy. It's easier than taking any practical action on them. Because the thing is this, most people want their fantasies to descend on them from heaven without any effort. They want it all to happen 'naturally', like some sudden miracle, just like they see in the movies.

The problem with this is that fantasies usually don't come by chance. (But when they do, savor them.) So what has to be done is to create the fantasy yourself. At first, this seems to kill the very idea of a natural fantasy because you have to deal with the mundane realities of the arrangements. Arrangements like the expenditure of 'hard earned' money and finding a willing Bond girl (a usual male fantasy) to go wading near the *Dr. No* waterfall in Jamaica with you. Much easier to pull out your *Dr. No* video and let 007 have the fun of that AGAIN, instead of you.

However, if you are special, a really special agent, the kind of guy that Charles Bronson talked about earlier who will "pick up the tab for that kind of living", you will turn off the video once you see Honey Rider wet down Bond to protect him from mosquitoes AGAIN, and get up from your sofa. You'll hit the internet and check out where that waterfall is. You'll print out your Q mission planner and start making a budget. You'll add up your money, you'll call up the appropriate girl, or set out to find one and you'll set a date.

"Oh, this is so mundane," you might think, "I don't want to manipulate this fantasy into being. I want it to happen naturally. Like I'm naturally there in Jamaica and I naturally meet a charming woman, and she naturally is free and wants to join me for a wade past the waterfall." But that's a lot of "naturals" to hope for, isn't it?

But, maybe you're the type that might get excited over a thing like this. Get excited over planning a Bond fantasy like this. Get excited about the challenge of it all and not get turned off by having to push this fantasy through like some mountain that you have to climb.

Now here is the main thing, the best part. Once you do get the woman who wants to go with you, and arrange the cash, the airline, the hotel, the passports, the week off from work and God knows what other things you'll need to do before you get anywhere near that waterfall, the fantasy will start to descend on you, start to envelop you. When you get to that waterfall with her, you'll look around at the beautiful scenery, see and feel the falls and see and feel the girl for real. Right then, all those arrangements you worked hard on will disappear from your mind. You will suddenly be surrounded by the fantasy, like Jimmy Stewart in *Vertigo* who manipulated his fantasy into being. You will look around, just like Stewart, with unbelievable fascination and the thought, "My God, this is really happening. I'm in the middle of the *Dr.*

No movie. And better than that, I don't have to deal with any villains. No, I don't. I just have to enjoy myself with my girl."

Remember, that when you create a wonderful fantasy like this, you should just enjoy it without destructive thoughts of, "But does this woman really like me, or is she only here for the free trip? And hell, this will be over in a couple of days and I'll be back at work. Oh, think of that big credit card bill I'm going to have. My friends will laugh at me when they hear how much I paid to pull this off."

Hey man, Mr. Field Agent, I won't laugh at you. Your friends that are following their dreams won't laugh at you. And the ones that aren't? Well, don't even bother to tell those guys, 'cause they wouldn't understand anyway. Besides, you'll be too busy planning your next fantasy. And you know what? You won't even bother to wait for the results of the next lottery, because you'll trust yourself to pull off your dreams, goals, fantasies and accomplishments – using your own visualization and action powers.

Now About That Bond Girl For The Waterfall

Perhaps she's a little harder to arrange than the airline tickets, but here's a little trick that might help you. It has to do with the idea that "need breaks iron". When you really need something you can hurdle all barriers. Here's a great case in point:

In Japan, on Christmas Eve, it's the custom for a guy to take his girl to a fancy dinner, give her an expensive gift and then take her to a fancy hotel. Because of this custom, hotels offer special holiday packages for a room and dinner for young couples. These hotels sell out by early November. One college guy I know reserved a room early for himself and his girlfriend. He had everything set up perfectly. That is, until she broke up with him. He was, of course, broken hearted. It was December 5th, but he could cancel the hotel package and get most of his money back. However, he decided to not cancel. He decided to hold the room, go for broke and find another girl to take there. So now he's twenty days and counting.

"Another three clicks ..."
Bond talking about the time bomb in *Goldfinger*

You'll notice that in most 007 movies, Bond has to deal with a countdown. A deadline. That's when he gets tough and gets down to business. And that's what makes the difference between people that are successful and in control of their lives, and ones that let circumstances control them.

Everyone has some natural talent in some field, but can they call up their talent at will? Can they produce on a deadline? Some people, when squeezed, fold. Others focus. That's what Bond does. He focuses. His survival instinct breaks down all barriers that are blocking him.

Likewise the guy with the Christmas hotel package and no date rose to the challenge of the deadline. He quickly found a new girl who was thrilled to go with him. And as Sinatra sings, "Ever since that night, they've been together." (Going on two years now.)

I'm not saying that this is the best way to get a girl, but it is a way to motivate yourself. I recommend that you start off with a little less extravagance, like buying some concert or event tickets in advance and then start searching for a date. Just a date, mind you, not the love of your life. But by doing that you can see if you will be able to focus and get an interesting girl to go to the event. This will also be a chance for you to practice what we covered earlier about acting like she is the love of your life as far as your relaxation and communication goes on the date.

Lesson learned: When you have a deadline, be like Bond. Call up your talent and deliver. When you're squeezed, focus. Do this by saying to yourself, "Need breaks iron."

Can I Actually Get The Thing I Want?

Ask yourself these questions about your goal to see if you can attract it into your life.

1. Does the thing you want exist? This is an obvious one, but sometimes people dream of things that don't exist—like a time machine to visit Cleopatra. Other times they just don't know that it exists, or believe that it exists. Like a job that is interesting. Or a relationship that is mostly harmonious. Or an affordable apartment that's in a clean and quiet neighborhood.

2. Is it right for you? Anything that adds to your lifestyle, that moves you to the next level of experience is right for you, as long as it doesn't take away or encroach on someone else's property.

3. Can you see yourself with it? Maybe you can imagine a great house, job, relationship, or experience, but you can't quite mentally put yourself into the picture because you can't believe you can achieve it. You believe other people can, but not you. Or maybe you don't believe that you deserve it. So work hard to imagine yourself standing in the middle of that desirable experience. Imagine the mission is accomplished with you in it.

4. Can your subconscious mind accept it? Again, this has to do with complete belief. You have to affirm, visualize and

take as much action as you can toward that goal until your subconscious can really see and believe that it's coming to you.

What's It Like To Be Rich?

Michael Caine was asked, "What's it like to be rich?" Now before I tell you his answer I have to tell you that I've been disappointed by wealthy people who have answered or avoided answering that question. Dr. Joyce Brothers, who I admire, was being interviewed on TV about her new book on money. After giving advice about how to acquire more money, she negated it by saying, "But after all, money is not so important as good health and good relationships." This sounds good, but in truth we know that money does buy health and good relationships. Good food, health clubs and medical treatment cost money. We need cash to maintain our health and it's a fact that most divorces are attributed to the couple's financial problems. Having money for life refreshing trips and entertainment for our mental health is good. Speaking of which, here are the four things that humans need to have good mental health:

1. To survive. As in having enough money for food and shelter.

2. To feel needed or important. Not movie star important, just important enough in their circle of friends.

3. To love and be loved. Family and even pets will do here.

4. Variety. Ah, the proverbial 'spice of life'. Without it our minds become bored and unbalanced.

Now back to wealthy people not fessing up to what it's like to be rich. Barbara Walters asked Arnold Schwartzenegger, "How do you feel making twenty million dollars a picture?" He rerouted the question with, "Well, the important thing is to always keep your value up like a rare stamp." This is true enough and I quote it elsewhere in this book as good advice. But he didn't answer the question. In fact, he avoided it.

When Johnny Carson's first ex-wife was asked how it felt to get all that divorce money, she answered directly to the audience that was wowing over the amount, "Listen, having a lot of money only means that you don't have to worry about money." Well, since Dale Carnegie said that, "Ninety percent of our worries are financial in nature," I would guess that not worrying about money is wonderful thing.

I could go on for a long time about wealthy people who dodge that question with a pat prepared answer, but now let's get to our hero Michael Caine who answered, "Being wealthy is great. Everyone should get their piece of it."

Get Your Piece of It

I want to expand on Michael Caine's statement; "Everyone should get their piece of it." I want you to ask yourself why you are going after a certain goal. Now as far back as the sixth grade I can remember my teacher telling us about the mule, the stick and the carrot. Every farm boy knows this. Humans are the same. They either go forward for enjoyment or to get away form an unpleasant experience.

But beyond that, what is motivating you toward your chosen goal? Do you want to be a successful singer because you like performing or is it a tool for you to be rich and famous? Do you want to be an actor because you like to be on the stage in front of people or is it a means to get money and attention? This is not to say that riches and fame are not a valid reasons. It's only to ask your reason. This is an important question because whatever you want to do, you can "get your piece of it."

There's not enough room at the top for everyone to be a famous recording star. But if it's the singing you like, there are thousands of local bands performing in nightclubs everywhere for you to sing with. There are local theatrical groups that put on plays where you can perform, so as to get your piece of the acting experience. It won't make you rich and famous unless lightning strikes and you get lucky, but you will always be able to perform in these kind of groups.

If you're just interested in going after the money then perhaps a more profitable way of doing it is advisable.

As for myself, I have always enjoyed the act of producing something since my school days. Be it my own *Twilight Zone* type magazine with my type-written stories, 8mm action movies filmed in my back yard, or theatrical movies. My main emphasis was getting my story produced and having it shown. This got me into some debt, because making money from them, even though I wanted that, took second place to getting my projects completed as best I could.

Later, I took a lesson from America's old train companies that failed to see that they were in the transportation business and not just in the train business. They didn't invest in trucks and airplanes and soon were left behind. So I expanded my area from just the feature film business to the communication business. I opened my mind to novel writing, acting, voice work, screenplay writing for others, seminar speaking and anywhere the communication business led me. Ultimately and happily, after some time, it led back to the feature film business.

So always remember Michael Caine's words, "Everyone should get their piece of it."

Take That First Step Now

"A journey of a thousand miles begins with one step" says an ancient Chinese proverb. "How do you eat an elephant? One bite at a time." Joke or proverb–take your pick–they're both true.

If you want to build a house, go to the lumberyard and buy a 2x4 to use on your house when it comes time to build. This is a powerful thing for the mind. I remember writing my first novel. The writing was fun and easy for me. The hard part was buying my first notebook to write it in.

The same goes for sit-ups to tighten the stomach. They're easy to do. The hard part is getting off the comfortable sofa and onto the floor. Olympic swimming champion Mark Spitz said, "Training your body is relatively easy. The hard part is getting your mind to call on your body to perform."

Maybe the hardest part of a mission for Bond is to leave Moneypenny's flirting, get out of the office and into his Aston Martin.

How To Materialize A Cadillac

The following is a true story: Fred started going to success/mind science classes in order to be more successful. He was unemployed at the time, but determined to improve his life.

The teacher of the class asked everyone to choose something to materialize. Fred chose a Cadillac and followed the teacher's regime for getting one. He cut out magazine photos of the type of Cadillac he wanted. He put them up on his apartment wall. He then read everything that he could about the car. He visualized the car at his meditative alpha level. He saw himself driving one in his mind and got into the happy feeling of it.

Then the teacher told him to go to a Cadillac dealership and sit in the car and take in the new car smell of a Cadillac to further program his mind. While he was doing this the manager of the dealership started talking with him. Fred was so enthusiastic about the car and telling the manager why it was so great with all the specific information, that the manager offered him a sales job.

The next day when the manager saw Fred drive up in his beat up old car he said to him, "You can't be seen driving that piece of junk. Pick out a Cadillac on the lot and it's yours."

There are many important lessons in this one true story. The main one is that the power of the universe works through people. Miracles happen, but not by a flash of light and magic. No, miracles happen through the law of attraction via people. Many people use the excuse for not taking action, by saying, "I can't be successful because it's who you know that counts." They're half-right. Get your mind prepared for success and start getting to know people that are associated with your goal so that the magic can happen. That way the law of attraction has a chance to work.

Your Power Bank

Well, maybe you don't have much money to get your dream started. But you can get a box or can to make a home savings bank for your goal. Cut out a photo from a magazine of your goal and paste it onto the bank. And when you're really frustrated because you can't get any forward action on your goal that day put ten dollars in your power bank. At least that's some action for the day. And it will affect your mind positively to come up with an idea for bigger action.

The Mission Planner

As mentioned before there are two tools that are essential for mission planning and accomplishment. The calendar for setting a start date. A date when you think is the best time to proceed. Or if it's a set time, like a convention, then you have to work with that date in mind. A mission with no date never happens.

The calculator will be used to make up your budget for the mission. This budget should include every possible expense that you can think of and also an amount of money for the unexpected. Now this 'unexpected' category is not for an emergency. You don't want to program your mind for that. This is for the unexpected good thing, like an extra attraction, side trip, or vacation extension.

To help you with this planning of schedule and budget I've has designed a 'Mission Planner' that you can get for free at my web site. Just go to 'Equipment' and print it out.

This mission planner has convenient printed boxes to write in all your required information such as airline, hotel and car rental reservation numbers. There are also boxes to write your credit card numbers, prepaid phone card numbers and important phone numbers. On the back side you can write more information. Then make a copy for your suitcase and also put the official hotel reservation paperwork in your suitcase.

This paper can be folded and put in your back pocket so that you can use it instead of having to pull out your wallet and address book constantly, searching for your information with your hands full of bags at the airport, for example. It will all be there on that one mission planner paper. Very Bond. Very Q. Get it now for free at www.BondLife.com. at 'Equipment'.

Budgeting For Your Dream

Whether it's a college education, a trip to Disneyworld, or a movie/dinner date with that important girl, you'll have to budget for it. What? Budget for just a movie date? You'd be surprised at how many guys right now would have to do just that in order to pull enough cash together for a simple night out. And millionaires right now are trying to figure out how to stretch their money to buy a condo off of New York's Central Park.

You'll find that when you are making up your budget, your dream is always bigger than your wallet. What to do? First cut down each individual item a little. If it's a trip, for example have a little less budgeted for restaurants. A little less for souvenirs. One day less for the rental car.

If this doesn't get you down to an affordable total, then cut one or two days off the trip. Do this instead of cutting down on the quality of your trip. Settling for a lower priced hotel should be avoided. I've often found myself budgeting for a long trip, say seven days, only to realize that five days is almost the same experience (especially with good event planning).

Be serious when budgeting. Get into it, but remember, even if you're short of your goal, budgeting should be an enjoyable experience. "A man's dream should exceed his reach, or what's a heaven for?"

Start With What You Have

You will usually find that you don't have quite enough money to meet the demands of your mission. So what do you do? To repeat, start with what you have. You'll find a space on the mission planner to write in how much cash and credit you have now. And then how much more you will earn by the time the mission date rolls around. The difference of your mission's budget and what you will totally have by the date, is the extra money that you will have to earn or find elsewhere. Or once again shave something off your budget without losing the quality of what you were going after in the first place.

Why There Are Obstacles To Your Goals

It's a world of inertia and friction. To get something done, energy applied in the right direction is needed. You can't get to the top of the mountain without energy. This is grade school stuff, of course.

But examine this. We humans have a great amount of mental and subconscious power. But this power would be wasted if there were no challenges to use that power on. It would be like having a souped up V-8 engine Jeep with four-wheel drive and then only going on flat smooth asphalt. What's all that power for?

The next time you ask yourself why you have all these challenges, let the answer be, "Because I have all this power."

A mission away from your personal base of operations will require you to set up a base elsewhere. Let's move forward to that.

9

HOTELS

Bond checks into a swanky hotel in almost all of his movies. He does this smoothly and with confidence. For guys that have been using the big resort hotels or went to them with their parents, it's no big deal. For guys that have been Motel Six-ing it for most of their lives, the larger hotels, especially the ones in Las Vegas can be pretty intimidating, even with the friendly service. Either way, I think, you'll find some unique tips here to smooth out your stay and make you look like you know what you're doing when you check in with your Bond girl or family. No man wants to be a Chevy Chase when dealing with a hotel. Every man wants to check in like Bond.

Bond: "Sorry about the accommodations, Contessa."
Tracy: "We should have rung ahead and booked."
OHMSS

That conversation took place as Bond and Tracy checked into a barn. What the heck, any port in a snowstorm. However, booking ahead is preferable for a smooth running trip. Easy to do, of course. And you've done it before. But always get the confirmation number and always have them fax or mail the confirmation letter to you. This near horror story will illustrate.

I was checking into a Hilton hotel once and the desk clerk couldn't find my name in the computer. "Do you have the confirmation number?" she smiled and asked.

"Sure," I said and pulled out a sheet of paper (Q's Mission Planner) that I had copied my entire itinerary onto and gave her the number.

"No, it's not here,"She said looking at the computer screen. Her smile ceased and she gave me a look that would have scared Oddjob. "And we're all sold out today." She learned her head over, looked past me to the next person in line, and said in a stern voice "Next."

Though taken slightly aback by her sudden change of demeanor, I was not daunted as I heard the James Bond theme song start twanging in my mind. I gave a slow smile as I slowly reached into my inside jacket pocket and withdrew my reservation on Hilton stationary and handed it gently and wordlessly to her. Her expression now turned into the same one Professor Dent had in *Dr. No* when he realized he had shot his six and Bond was fully loaded.

She took the paper, went into the back office, and came out with the head clerk who arranged an upgraded room for me for the same price quoted on their stationary.

Thank God I had gotten into the habit of 'loading' my jacket with the next hotel confirmation paper that I usually pack into my luggage as a back up. Otherwise I would have been forced to find a barn like Bond and Tracy.

From that time on when checking in, instead of giving them my name, I just hand them their confirmation letter and let them find me in the computer while I glance around the lobby and take in the action.

If you book hotels on the internet, always print out the confirmation number page to use when checking in.

Remember to take Tracy's advice. Book ahead and have the confirmation letter in your pocket.

"I'll Thank You Exactly One Hundred Times"

If a hotel that you absolutely need is all booked up, here's a technique that you can use to get a room in that sold out hotel.

1. Tell the person on the phone in charge of reservations to put your name on the waiting list.

2. Give them your name and credit card number. (The credit card number is important here.)

3. Ask the person on the phone for their name.

4. Tell the person that "If I do get a room, I'll find you at the hotel and thank you exactly one hundred times."

5. They will call you back with a room for sure.

6. When you arrive at the hotel, find that person and give them an envelope with one hundred dollars in it.

Now as I said, this technique is used when you absolutely must have a room in that hotel. You won't need to do this often. But just having this technique in mind will give you the confidence you need to know that any hotel is yours for the asking.

Beware the Hotel Computer

Some people like to put advance cash on their room when checking in so that not as much money is charged to their credit card. If you are approaching your credit limit you may have to do this. Try to avoid it, if possible. Computer technology is getting pretty fool proof, but the people operating them are still human and can make mistakes. I recently asked a Las Vegas front desk clerk if it was advisable to put some of my winnings against my room. He said, "I wouldn't. Sometimes the computer gets screwed up."

Likewise, if your Bond girl checks in before you and uses her credit card, do not have the desk clerk switch it over to your card when you arrive. If he makes a mistake both you and your girl may have the same day charged to both of your cards. If he makes a big mistake, your whole stay could be charged to both of your cards. You don't want to spend a lot of time on the phone once you get back home trying to correct the mistake.

Always use one card only, even if it's your girl's card. Pay her the cash equivalent when you get the final bill. Never put any extra cash against your room unless you're approaching your credit limit and need the credit for the rest of your trip.

To Valet Or Not To Valet

Always use the valet parking. Why? Visualize this: You've got your Bond girl in the car and your Vegas hotel is just up ahead."Look there it is," she says excitedly."I can't wait to see the room.Will we gamble first, or eat or what?"

You're thinking "Or what" as you pull into the large entrance area. You notice that all the spaces of the giant front parking area are taken.You see the valets waiting for you right by the front door, but quickly think "Why let a stranger drive my car and park it who knows where? Why should I have to tip him two bucks and tip the bellhop who takes the bags out of the car, and then the other bellhop that takes the bags to the room? That's six bucks! I can do it all myself and save the money for the casino. Let's see. Six bucks is twenty-four quarters. That's a lot of chances to possibly win the 'Mega Bucks' jackpot."

Not thinking to drop your girl off at the front door and give her some gambling money to kill time with, you proceed with her up into the parking structure. You spiral dizzyingly upward as you see that the first five levels are reserved for valet parked cars only. "I'm getting nauseous from the winding around and the car fumes," she says with her hand over her mouth.

"Just a few more levels," you assure her, as you are now getting desperate to find a space for your car before she messes up the interior. "Ah, there's one," but another car comes out of nowhere and beats you to it.

Finally on the tenth floor you get it parked. "Ok, let's check in," you encourage. You get your bags out of the trunk. They feel like they have five sacks of quarters in them. "What does she have in there for three nights?" you ask yourself, but are smart enough not to let it escape your lips. "Where's the elevator?"

"I don't know," she replies like it's not her problem and you both know it.

Dodging both the upcoming and down going cars you

wheel your suitcases around the structure until you get to the elevator. Of course, both the wait and the ride are long because it stops on every floor to pick up the other non-Bond types loaded with suitcases and dreaming about the twenty-four quarters saved.

The elevator arrives on the lobby level. But where is the lobby? Oh no, you have to wheel through another parking lot just to get to the main building and the air conditioning. Finally you enter into what seems to be a back entrance by holding the door open with your shoulder. And yes, it is a back entrance, with people heading to the nearby restrooms. Ah, a sign pointing to the front desk. Where is it? Clear over on the other side of the football field size casino with gamblers walking ever which way clinging to their buckets of quarters. "Did they win them by gambling with the money they saved by not using the valet?" you wonder.

Approaching the front desk the bell captain eyes your luggage, but you avoid eye contact and push your luggage in line for the next available desk clerk. Where's your girl? You turn around and she's not there. Did she go to the restroom? Is she playing a slot machine? Then the morbid thought occurs to you that she's probably run off with some guy who wastes his money on things like valet parking.

"Your baggage, Sir"
"In the boot," Bond says. "And take care of those clubs."
"Right, Sir."
From *OHMSS*

Now that's the way to check into a hotel. Especially a large crowded one. You pull your car up to the big showy entrance with your girl taking in the sight with a big smile. Valets open the car doors for both you and her. "Checking in, Sir?"

"Yes, I am," you answer taking the ticket stub from the valet and putting it securely in your wallet so it won't get lost with all the other paperwork that you'll be getting.

You don't want the guy telling you that he'll only take the luggage in the door and a bellhop will get it to your room. He does that to the Clydes who don't know that they should tip him there. You know it and tip him right there. He gives you another ticket for your luggage. You put that into your wallet as well and then take your girl by the hand and lead her into the lobby like Bond escorting Sylvia Trench. Since you don't have to worry about your car or luggage, you can concentrate on that enjoyable experience.

"But is my car safe with the valet?"

I get asked that a lot at seminars and I think the answer is clear. Your car will be parked in the valet parking area where the valets are constantly running back and forth. This would encourage a car thief to go to the other areas of the parking lot or structure for their caper.

Also, your car is insured and all your valuables are in your suitcase. You would never leave anything valuable in the car. The valets are experienced at driving all kinds of cars, so feel safe with your car in their hands. Safer, in fact, than if you had parked it up on the tenth floor.

The other really Bond thing about the valet service is that you can call from your room to the valet to get your car and have it waiting for you by the time you leave your room, go down the elevator and out to the front entrance. You will walk your girl outside where she will see your car waiting with both doors open and your valet standing by to close them once you get in. Very 007. All for only a few bucks tip.

Your room key, Mr. Bond

We talked about this a little already, but the main thing to remember is that rooms are not assigned until you check in. Even though you may have requested your preference such as a non-smoking room, high floor, pool view, it's up to the clerk at check in to find the room for you. The earlier the check-in time, the better your chances of getting the type of room you want. However, if the price of the room you choose includes a special amenity, then you will have that special room held for you. Just remember that at check in, you start all over again trying for the room you want. Your requests merely show up on the clerk's computer. If the clerk checks around on the computer for various rooms for you and you get what you want, a tip is always appreciated, but not necessary.

Special note: If you make your reservations on the internet, the hotel web site will often tell you the exact type of room you will get (usually with a photo) and if it's a higher or lower floor, depending on the price. For example, the Hilton does this with their web site reservations.

Now let's continue with the check-in process. The front desk is where they load you down with papers such as your room card keys in an envelope, your receipt, map of the hotel, special deals and so on. Just be sure to put your card key in your front pocket inside your money clip or in your wallet so you don't lose it amongst all the papers.

For security reasons your room number will not be on the card keys, it will be written on the small envelope that has your card keys in them. You should tear off the piece that has your room number written on it and put it in your wallet. The reason to do this is that with the larger hotels that have thousands of rooms as the ones in Las Vegas do, your room number will be something like this: 71425. With all the excitement of your trip and the day's activities, it's a cinch you'll forget it. So now you've got the room number in your wallet.

The bellhop will take you to your room with your luggage in smaller hotels. For the larger ones, you go to your room and then call down with the ticket number that they gave you upon arrival. Your bags will come up in about ten minutes with a brand new bellhop to tip.

"Thank you Gentlemen for such a sterling service."
Bond in *Diamonds Are Forever*

In the very first Bond movie *Dr. No*, we see 007 sitting at the baccarat table playing against Miss Trench. When he gets up to leave he casually leaves a tip for the dealers. When he walks out the front door, he even more casually gives a tip to the doorman. Thus, tipping and tipping with style is part of Bond's inherent manner and must be learned, even if it's only to impress the Bond girl on your arm. As we proceed you'll find that there's more to tipping than using it to merely impress and create an image for yourself.

To Insure Promptness, is where the word tip came from. There is customary tipping and tipping for extra service. You should do both.

The Five Levels Of Tipping

I'm excited to say that I came up with these levels all by myself when I began to make a case for tipping, after hearing all the reasons not to tip. Reasons ranging from, "They get a salary, so why should I have to tip?" To, "Why does society say tip waitresses who are serving food and not fast food service employees? I don't want to play society's games." The variety of reasons to not tip usually come from people fearful of not having enough money in the future, so they hold on to every dollar, even on an expensive vacation. Let's face it, some that make a case for not tipping are just downright cheap.

I myself have never been in a job that has customary tipping, so I'm not coming from the point of view of defending services that are tipped. I just watched and listened to see what was cool and what was not.

Here's what I came up with as the five levels of tipping:

1. You tip because it's the custom. (This is an OK reason.)

2. You tip because you want to be cool like Bond. (A fun reason.)

3. You tip to evoke the law of circulation, so that your money comes back to you 10 times. (A great prosperity technique.)

4. You tip because you used to have a job like that person and appreciate the hard work that goes into that job. (A very human reason.)

5. You tip because you realize that the energy animating that person is the same energy that is in you and animating you. (A spiritual reason.)

Who To Tip, When, Where and How Much

For restaurant waitresses fifteen to twenty percent is the norm. Give bellhops a couple of dollars a bag, with a five-dollar bill doing it well in expensive hotels. Again, don't forget that the bellhop outside the hotel will be a different one than the guy bringing your bag upstairs so tip him when you get inside the lobby or get it over with right at the car. Two or three bucks will do him nicely. Your valet parking attendant should get three dollars because he has to be responsible for your car. Tip the same when he brings it out for you.

In a casino, drinks are free if you're gambling, but tip the waitress one or two dollars. Most of those girls are visiting chiropractors for leg and back problems. If a change girl guides you to a good machine you can tip her on a big win if you like.

I think an important person to tip in a hotel is the unseen maid that has to make those giant beds and clean your room. A couple of dollars left on the pillow is always appreciated. Lots of these women are single parents and could use the money. As for me, making a bed has been a drag since childhood, so the maid has got my vote of support.

Outside the hotel the doorman that calls you a taxi should get a few bucks. The ones that only open the door for a waiting taxi should get a dollar. The way I figure it is that (especially in Las Vegas where I'm gambling many dollars) tipping is part of the fun. At the very least your date will see you tipping and appreciate the style and prosperity of it.

"What's the largest tip you ever got?"

Everyone agrees that Frank Sinatra was the best tipper to ever come along. He once asked a parking valet what the biggest tip he ever got was. The valet said it was a hundred dollars. So Sinatra gave him two hundred dollars. As he got in his car Sinatra asked him "Who gave you the hundred dollar tip?" The valet replied "You did."

Whoops! Out Of Small Bills?

This can happen if you've been using your ones and fives to pay for small items. It's important to always use twenties to pay for things so that you get back ones and fives and keep them in your left pocket for use when you're in a situation where you will tip a lot, like checking into a hotel.

Now if you're checking in and you need to tip and you find that you only have large bills on you, fear not. Just look at the nametag of the bellhop or parking valet, smile and say "Thanks Bob, I'll take care of you later." The front desk will always make change for you and then you can find that bellhop or valet and tip him with a "Thanks again, Bob."

Congratulations. You're In Your Room

You've tipped the bellhop and he leaves. You remembered to say, "This room will do us nicely." Now what? That's easy. You unpack and enjoy whatever attraction you came there for. If she's in the same room with you, you can give her a few minutes to freshen up and then go out. If she's in another room, tell her to call you when she's ready.

Don't Miss This Part

Here's a biggie, but I don't want to dwell on it for too long. Always carry some stick incense in your luggage with a cigarette lighter tied to the box with a rubber band. This way you don't have to fool with matches. A lighter is much safer and easier to use.

Every time you use the restroom, light an incense stick. After you're finished, put it out. This will keep the air fresh.

You don't want your girl coming in there next without a pleasing aroma. For that matter, you should use this at home, even if you live alone.

Because hotels consider incense 'smoking material' you shouldn't use it in the room if yours is designated for non-smoking, which is the type of room you should be in anyway. It's fine to use it in the bathroom with the blower on.

Now I guarantee what's going to happen to you. You'll be in the bathroom with your girl waiting to use it next and you'll say to yourself "Oh yeah, that Bond lifestyle guy told me to get some incense and I forgot about it." So get that box of incense and lighter soon and put them in your luggage so that it's there when you need it. Put another set in your home restroom.

While we're on the subject of your home restroom, remove the magazines from there when you have a female guest over, or any guest for that matter. You don't want them to see the magazines and visualize you sitting on the john reading them. Remember: image, image and image.

Case in point: Once two actresses came over to my apartment to see themselves in a movie I was editing there. Before they arrived I cleaned up the place and threw the book that was next to the toilet into my private sauna that was connected to the restroom. The girls viewed their scenes and did use the restroom. Later, driving them to lunch, one girl said to the other "Did you see his sauna in his restroom? He sits in there and reads his book."

Now there's an image. Me sitting in my private sauna reading a book. Prosperity, health and intellectual reading. Much better those actresses imagining me ... well, I don't even want you to imagine me reading anywhere but in my private sauna.

Room Service

A lot of women think room service is the height of class. Probably due to the popularity of the movie *Pretty Woman*. You can order food or the Richard Gere special of strawberries and champagne. Do room service once for your girl and see how it goes over. The champagne list will at first look scary with one to five hundred dollar bottles listed. If this is out of your league, you can order the hotel brand for twenty dollars. It's delivered on ice with two glasses and looks great. Not a bad price to give her the Julia Roberts experience.

Now a big word of warning: if you are in your room alone and put out the room service tray in the hall, be sure to not let the door close behind you because it will lock automatically. Don't feel too bad if that happens and you have to get another key. You won't be the first guy to go down to the lobby in his Fruit of the Looms.

They Want You To Have A Great Time

Always remember that no matter how large the hotel, they want you to have a good stay there so that you'll return and also tell your friends what a great place it is. Don't be afraid to ask them for help, for advice, to arrange a tour, airline reservations or show tickets. They are there to help. Go to the front desk or the customer service counter and ask.

Now speaking of hotels, here's a little city that has the ten largest hotels in the world.

LAS VEGAS

The reason I include this city in the desert in this book is that Las Vegas is the easiest place to live the James Bond lifestyle and also the easiest place to entertain anyone. The reason being that all the entertainment is right in front of you. You need no imagination to think of things to do. Check out *100 Things to Do In Las Vegas* on my web site on the *00 Agents* page. The reason that everything is comparatively inexpensive is that the casino hotels need to attract people into the desert for gambling, because that's how they make their money. Because of that hotel rooms, food and entertainment (a lot which is free) is inexpensive. Put Las Vegas on your list as an important place to take your Bond girl, be it in the same or separate rooms.

Stay In a Castle, a Palace, a Pyramid or a Circus

There are two great areas that I recommend as the best place to stay. The first is the intersection where the Tropicana, MGM, New York New York, Luxor and Excalibur Hotels are all together. For a spectacular view stand in front of the Tropicana Hotel and look over at the skyline of the New York New York Hotel. Then go up to the middle of the cross walk and look down the strip toward the Eiffel Tower of the Paris Hotel. Wow! What a sight!

The other area to stay at is the Caesars, Mirage, Flamingo and Treasure Island Hotel area. Don't take your girl to the nearby Imperial Palace Hotel, except to see the car museum. The Imperial Palace is inexpensive and perfectly located, but packed with noisy tour groups, noisy air conditioners and narrow windowed views of the parking lot. How do I know? A buddy invited me there. I had a great time, but was hardly in the room ... thank God.

For hotel selection you should take a look at a site on the internet that has current prices and great color photos of the rooms and then make your plans. Here I will give you my personal observations.

For uniqueness and fun with a fair price try the pyramid shaped Luxor Hotel. The elevators run at a thirty-six degree angle up the edges of the pyramid. You walk to your room via a balcony style walkway that looks down into the Egyptian wonder of the place which is so large that nine 747 jumbo jets could fit in it. Four on the bottom, three in the middle and two on top. The buffet has a wonderful pyramid interior ambience, and the ride on the attraction floor called *Search for the Obelisk* is great. By the way, an obelisk is a tall four sided stone pillar tapering to its pyramid shaped top. Just in case your girl asks you.

At the other great area, Caesars Palace is the place to stay with their great shopping mall and 3D-ride attraction called *Race for Atlantis*. The price is a tad higher, but well worth it.

As for Vegas hotel prices, Sunday through Thursday nights are much cheaper with Friday and Saturday nights about fifty percent more. However, when there is a convention or an event like championship boxing, all the regular prices go out the window and every hotel becomes weekend priced. But still good value.

Be aware also that the hotels advertise "no Saturday arrivals." However, that's mostly to keep the tour companies from booking up lots of rooms on that day. If it's just one room and you plan on staying a couple of days, they'll always waive the no Saturday arrival rule for you. Sometimes the reservation person will call their boss and sometimes, especially if you're going to stay five or more days, they don't. So never give up on a "no Saturday arrivals notice." If this fails you can start Saturday night at a smaller hotel and them move up on Sunday. If you can do it, arrive on a Sunday and stay till Friday afternoon. This way you'll have fewer crowds and less hotel expense.

The Las Vegas Hilton (known as The International during Elvis's days) has the not-to-be-missed *Star Trek Attraction* with its interesting *Trek* museum that leads to a fantastic ride. How they beam you up to a real star ship is beyond me. Maybe it just hovers over Las Vegas waiting for passengers.

Tournament of Kings - EFX - Splash

These are the three best shows for my money in Vegas now, with *Tournament of Kings* at the Excalibur being one of the few remaining dinner shows. You'll see knights jousting on horses, special effects, battles and then circus acrobats. All while you're eating your Cornish hen with your fingers. All the seats in this arena are good, so no need to worry about what seat you'll get if you buy your tickets at the last minute.

The *EFX* show at the MGM has forty million dollars worth of production value on the stage, and you'll see every dollar of it. Two fire breathing dragons and a re-enactment of *The Time Machine* with a great 3D time travel sequence will keep your date well entertained. The tickets are high priced, but worth it. Get your tickets early and asked for seats on the raked (slanted) floor and not at the flat tables where your view is blocked by someone's head.

The *Splash* show at the Riviera has lower priced tickets and a superb variety show of singers, dancers, ice skaters, comedians and four motorcyclists who speed around the inside of a steel ball.

There are a lot of other great shows that you should check out. If the ticket prices bother you, just think how much you'll be saving while you're away from the slot machines and crap tables. In fact, the casino bosses know this. Which is why they always got angry with Sammy Davis Jr. when his show went over an hour. They didn't want to have all their high rollers sitting in the show room watching Sammy do his six gun-twirling act when they should be out in the casino rolling them bones.

The Canyon - Lake Mead - The Dam

If you're planning to drive to the Grand Canyon to stay overnight, making reservations to stay at one of the hotels right next to it would be a good idea. They are the El Tovar, Thunderbird and Kachina hotels. All three are right on the edge of the canyon, so don't wake up there on the proverbial 'wrong side of the bed'.

Be sure to wake your girl up before sunrise and walk the horseshoe rim to the left that goes to the other side of the canyon. It only takes forty minutes and the two of you will feel like Adam and Eve on a newly born earth.

If it's just a day trip you're interested in you can go to the Canyon from Vegas by air, tour bus or car. I've heard so many complaints about how bad the air trip tour is that I've avoided it. Complaints are always about a very rough, uncomfortable and nauseating flight where many passengers get sick and ... well, you *can* imagine.

I recommend the bus tour. It's about one hundred eighty dollars for two people. They pick you up at your hotel, give you a narrated tour past homes of some celebrities, and visit Hoover Dam for a quick exterior look then drive through the desert on a four-hour trip to the canyon. You stop for lunch, which is included in your tour price, then go on to the canyon. Your bus stops at three points for about forty minutes each and then its back to Vegas. The whole trip takes thirteen hours, but it's the best way to go on a day trip. Saying that, however, I'd recommend that you rent a car, stay one night, get up before sunrise and walk the rim before breakfast.

The tour companies also offer a combination Hoover Dam tour and Lake Mead cruise on a paddlewheel boat. The price is sixty dollars for two. You get a twenty minute interior tour of the dam and then an hour long cruise on the lake. The red rock mountains are beautiful against the dark blue waters. This is a great outing and great value for the seven hour round trip from your hotel and back.

You may also consider other tours into the desert or Monument Valley. Tours are a great way to add variety to your Las Vegas experience.

Amusements

Young or old can enjoy the variety of amusement parks, water parks, rides and attractions on the Vegas strip. For a quick mention don't miss: (to repeat) *The Star Trek Attraction*, the Fremont Street light show, *Race for Atlantis* at Caesars Palace, Luxor's *Search for the Obelisk*, Treasure

Island's *Pirate Ship Battle* and the Mirage volcano eruption.

A good way of enjoying your day in Vegas is to have breakfast, take a tour, do some hotel hopping, take a swim, see a show and then do some gambling at night.

The Dangerous Strip

Well, Bugsy Siegal and the boys have long since given the Vegas strip over to the corporations. Now there are so many security men and cameras watching the hotels and casinos that crime is non-existent there. Bicycling policemen patrol the exterior strip. Except for pickpockets at the outdoor shows, such as the pirate ship battle, the streets are safe. However, there is a big danger on the strip. So beware, and protect your Bond girl from it.

The big danger is that after the outside shows are finished there are large crowds pushing their way in various directions, so that once a month someone is pushed into the street and hit by a passing car. So, stay away from the street side of the sidewalk, no matter how crowded it is, or how much in a hurry you are to get to the next attraction.

The Luxor area that I recommended has escalator cross walks on all four corners of that intersection. However, the other areas (for the most part) have the pedestrians crossing the actual street. This is a dangerous situation with cars making speedy weird turns and crowds not waiting for the green pedestrian crossing light. Whatever you do don't cross with them. Wait for your green light and you and your date just might have a chance of surviving the cross.

So, the biggest dangers of the strip? Cars and pickpockets. That is as long as you're not addicted to gambling. Which brings us to the number one reason that there is a town in the middle of the desert to begin with.

CASINO GAMBLING

Bond is first seen on the screen in *Dr. No* playing baccarat. He's playing the same game in *Thunderball* and *OHMSS*. He plays craps in *Diamonds Are Forever*, and then backgammon in *Octopussy*. Thus we often associate him with games of chance, besides his chancy occupation. It has been often echoed by casino managers that "the reason men come to Las Vegas is so they can be James Bond." Yes, there are the luxury hotels and swimming pools stocked with beautiful women. But there is also gambling. The important thing about gambling as far as this course is concerned is that women, for the most part, love to gamble. They love those machines and, though they don't usually play craps, once you get them to the table they love to 'roll them bones.'

You can learn the ins and outs of the different games from gambling books and videos. So I will stick with just the special techniques and mindset, as far as it pertains to us doing a 007 at the casino and how to entertain your 'Plenty O'Toole' when you take her there.

Gambling - Gaming - Entertainment

In the Casino business the word 'gambling' was (of course) used. To soften the idea and get it away from the cellar crap game image, the casino publicists came up with the word 'gaming'. After a few years it was softened again to 'entertainment'. If you keep that word in mind, you can always win. Here's how you do it:

On the Mission Planner budget, you'll see a space for "casino". This is where you put the amount of money you intend to 'entertain' yourself and your date with. Yes, it is your gambling budget. Now let's define who you are and what you're doing in the casino. If you are going there to have a good time with your date by playing the machines at various casinos, trying out roulette, blackjack and baccarat, or to give your date a quick thrill by playing a few dollars on the big wheel, then you are there to 'game'. However, if you are there to win enough money to pay your bills, get out of debt, to finance a new car or change your life, then you are GAMBLING.

If you are there to gamble, then don't think that you are doing anything else but that. Just remember that the house always has the mathematical advantage (called 'the house edge') and will always win in the long run. What gamblers hope for are moments when those mathematical odds go out the window and there is a steak of good luck. This also goes the other way when a streak of bad luck comes. What serious gamblers do is bet low with their own money, so that the losing streak doesn't hurt them so much. When they are ahead and have some of the casino's money in their pocket they bet big, hoping for a long hot streak.

By the way, I've seen freelance guys trying to make their money both at gambling and at the stock market, buying and selling quickly in order to 'make a killing'. You can guess who got killed, as these guys are now like the song says, "parking cars and pumping gas." Quite literally I'm afraid. As far as the stock market goes, if you're sure that a stock will go up, always remember that the guy who is selling it to you and who has the same information as you, is just as sure that the same stock will go down. Enough said.

How To Always Win Like Bond

Bond girls are impressed when you always win. That's because they see you as a winner and you see yourself as a winner. Now here's how to do it.

The money that you've allotted for your casino budget should be considered already gone, just like the money you will use for the hotel, food, shows, taxis and tips. It's gone. It is slated for your entertainment. Not for you to hold onto. Not for you to 'invest' in gambling. But for you to enjoy the casino.

If you stay on budget in the casino for your trip, or even under budget, then you've won. You and your date were entertained within that budget. You're a winner. Just like you wouldn't come out of a good show and say, "Hey, I lost the price of admission" or eat at a good restaurant and say, "Ah hell, I lost my money." No. Not if you were entertained and well fed, you wouldn't. So if you 'lose' you say, "Wow! That was fun." You can even quote James Coburn in *Hard Times* saying "My Mama told me that the next best thing to playing and winning, is playing and losing." Meaning, not playing at all is number three.

About forty percent of the time you will actually be financially ahead if you play with your head and the idea just to survive as long as you can on your casino 'entertainment' allowance.

Start Your Casino Date Off Like Bond

007 walks into the casino with his date. He chooses a comfortable area with some fun looking slot machines and says, "Let's play in this area for a while. What machine looks good to you?" She chooses one and sits down. Before she can open her purse Bond already has his money clip out and slips a twenty into her machine.

"I have gambling money," she says.

"I know," he says very casually "that's for starters." With his own theme song twanging in his mind he chooses a machine near her and starts his play.

"Twenty dollars?" you say. "I gotta give her twenty dollars?" Well, think of it this way. When she gets home she'll tell all her friends and relatives that a couple of times you started off her gambling that way. That's a lot of image advertising for just a couple of twenties. Not to mention how you'll outrank all the tightwads and less thoughtful guys she used to date.

"But I Don't Like To Gamble"

What she means is that she doesn't like to risk her money and lose the money that she wants to use for shopping. That's okay, because here's what you'll do. (This is the only devious thing in the book.) If your Bond girl is squeamish about risking her money or even your money, this is the way to loosen her up to the gaming experience.

But first one special note: If she has religious reasons for not gambling then never suggest she gamble. If it's a problem for her if you gamble then stay away from it and enjoy the other attractions.

Okay, having said that, let's get back to being devious. Wait until your reluctant gambler is out of sight and hearing range, like when she goes to the restroom, then slip a one hundred-dollar bill into your machine. The bell will start dinging as the machine gives you credit for the cash. Then once it's finished resume your play. When your date comes over hit the 'cash out' button and the machine will start spitting out all those coins. "Wow! You won all that?" She'll ask. "Yeah, I hit a few small jackpots" you'll answer. Then the clincher: "So let's have fun gambling on the house's money."

Now just fill up a coin bucket and give it to her to take to the change booth to get it counted and changed to bills. Don't help her carry it. She'll love all that weight. When she comes back with the cash, take half of it and say something like, "Let's win some more using the casino's money." You'll probably see your reluctant gambler turn into a slot machine animal.

Plenty: "Say, you played this game before."
Bond: "Just once."
Diamonds Are Forever

Now it's time to get her on the crap table and let her handle 'them bones.' For starters you can tell her that the ancient Greeks made dice out of goat's bones to predict their next season's success with their crops. Hence the expression 'bones'. It is also true that archaeologists at the Pompeii diggings found loaded dice from that ancient time. Can you imagine the disappointment of the owner of those dice? He's on a big winning streak using the crooked dice and then Mt. Vesuvius erupts. He probably thought God was telling him to go straight.

First find a crap table where you can get a comfortable space with some elbowroom for her to throw. Most of the tables now have five-dollar minimum pass line bets, and since any three-dollar table will be packed, you'll have to play at the five dollar ones.

One hundred dollars would be a good amount to buy chips for the two of you. It's much more expensive than the slots, but you won't be playing here too much or too long, unless you get a lucky streak going.

Place your cash on the table, as the dealers are not allowed to take it from your hand. In addition, chip handling between the player and the dealer is made only on the table. The one hundred dollars will give you ten chips apiece to play with. Plenty to survive for a while and give her some fun.

The 'pass line' bet in craps is the best bet in the casino with the house advantage only a small 1.4 percent. This mentally gives you an almost 50/50 bet. Wait for the 'come out roll' to be called. The dealer will say loudly "Coming out". This starts a new game. Each of you will put a five dollar chip on the pass line. Now here comes the easy part, if you are a beginner. Just wait. If the dealer yells "Winner" and puts another five dollar chip next to your original bet, you've won. Pick up the chips, or just take one and leave one on the pass line for the next come out. If the dealer says, "Line away" (they never say "loser") and takes your bet, you've lost. So be ready to place another chip down on the pass line for the next game. Simple. Now you're a craps player.

Here's what really happened. It's simple for the pass line. On the 'Come out' roll, if the 'shooter' rolls a 7 or 11, all the pass line betters win. If he rolls a 2, 3, or 12 on the first roll, all the pass line betters lose. If he rolls any of the remaining numbers (4, 5, 6, 8, 9 or 10) called 'the numbers'; a marker is placed on that number on the table. Then the shooter must roll that number again before he rolls a 7. Thus on the come out roll a 7 is a winner, after that a 7 is a loser. That's all there is to it on the pass line. Easy to understand and easy to explain to your date.

Only make bets when the dice are in the middle of the table. When they are there the stickman will have control of them with his stick and the action has momentarily stopped.

If you watch for awhile, standing back from the table or even by making a pass line bet when others do, you'll get the feel of table etiquette right away.

When Do You Throw the Dice?

Everyone gets a chance to throw the dice. The rotation goes around the table clockwise. A player keeps throwing until he '7s out' (loses) and then the player on his left gets his turn to throw.

Now, here's a strategy that you won't find in any book. When you or your date are not throwing the dice make the minimum pass line bet and enjoy the game until the dice come to you. (You should be to the right of your girl so that you throw first and she can gain confidence by watching you as you explain what's going on.) When you get the dice, that's your chance to make more varied bets, to increase the action and fun for yourself. Thus your date watches you throw, place various bets, and make call bets with the dealers. You'll look like 007 himself with all that action.

Do the same when she is throwing also. Then when she loses the dice, you can go back to the pass line minimum bets until you get those 'bones' back. Naturally, this will slow down your betting and your losses, giving you more time on the table to enjoy the game. Alternatively, as I sometimes do, you can collect your winnings, tip the dealers and bid a hasty retreat with your winnings (or cut your losses).

If you win, maybe your date will repeat Plenty O'Toole's line: "You handle those cubes like a monkey handles coconuts."

The Dice Comes To You

When the player to your immediate right loses, a new game will start with you 'shooting' the dice. The dealer will say "New shooter coming out." With his stick he will push six dice in front of you on the table. After making your pass line bet, hesitate a moment to see if the players have finished betting, then throw them to the other end of the table. You must hit the wall at the other end. If you don't, it's okay the first time, but the dealer will politely tell you to do so. Also remember to handle the dice with one hand and keep that hand above the table. Obviously, a rule to discourage switching dice.

Your date will watch you and learn. When it's her turn to throw you can quietly talk her through it if she shows hesitation. If she's confident, keep quiet and let her have fun. If the table gets noisy with cheering you can join in with encouragement of your own. In craps it's everyone against the dice, so a noisy camaraderie develops, making craps a truly entertaining game.

When one of you is shooting, this is the time to start making more and varied bets to increase as I mentioned. Here are two extra bets that will give you a lot of action and make you look like you know what you're doing. Which you will.

The Come Bet

The 'come' bet box is clearly marked on the table next to the pass line. This bet works exactly like the pass line. You can place a bet there anytime and start a new game of your own which follows the pass line rules. 7 or 11 on the first roll you win. 2, 3, or 12 on the first roll, you lose. If a number comes up on this starting roll (4, 5, 6, 8, 9 or 10) the dealer will take your bet off the come

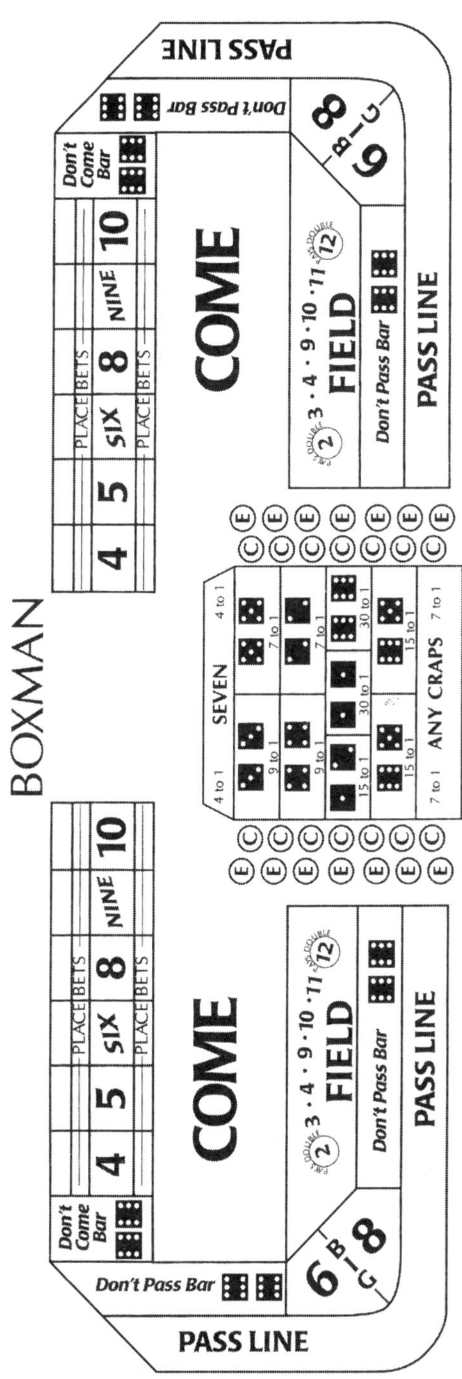
BOXMAN
PASS LINE
Don't Pass Bar
Don't Come Bar
PLACE BETS
4
5
SIX
8
NINE
10
COME
2
3 · 4 · 9 · 10 · 11
12
FIELD
PAYS DOUBLE
Don't Pass Bar
PASS LINE
BIG 6 8
SEVEN
4 to 1
9 to 1
7 to 1
15 to 1
30 to 1
ANY CRAPS
7 to 1
C
E

space and place it on that number. (It 'comes' to that number). If that number comes up before a 7 you win. If the 7 is thrown first you lose. You can make bets on the 'comes' after each roll, if you like, giving you a lot of action for your roll. Soon you'll have money on many numbers. Every time one of those numbers comes up the dealer will pay you. Beware though; when a 7 comes you lose all those bets.

By the way, even though you may be making other bets, you must always make a pass line bet to throw the dice.

The Hard Ways

This was one of the bets that Bond made in *Diamonds Are Forever*. ("Two hundred on the hard way.") Hard way numbers are easy to see because they are matching numbers on the dice. A hard four is 2-2 (soft is 3-1). A hard six is 3-3 (soft is 5-1, 4-2). A hard 8 is 4-4 (soft is 6-2, 5-3). A hard ten is 5-5 (soft is 6-4). To really make it easy they are pictured as dice in the middle of the table layout with the odds next to them. The hard 6 and hard 8 pay nine dollars for every dollar bet. The hard 4 and hard 10 pay seven dollars for every dollar bet.

And to make it even easier the stickman always calls out "Ten the hard way" or "Ten, easy ten." And it's up to the stickman to pay you, so once you get your bet down on a hard way number, your pay out (or loss) is automatic.

The house has a bigger edge on the hard ways: 9.1 percent on the 6 and 8, and 11.1 percent on the 4 and 10. That doesn't matter so much in short term, hit and run play, because the great thing about making hard way bets is this: (this is not in books) You don't have to bet the table minimum of five dollars on them. You can bet one dollar. Of course, you will have your pass line bet down, but now you only risk a dollar on the hard ways. When you lose by a 7 coming up, or the 'easy way' of that number coming up, you just lose a dollar. When you win, the stickman taps his stick on the table near you and says to the dealer "Pay this man nine dollars" or "Pay this man seven dollars". Only you (and other hard way betters) are pointed out and paid, making you look special to your date.

To make a 'hard way' bet, just toss a chip in the center of the table in the direction of the 'hard way' spaces and call out "a hard eight" or "a hard ten." The dealer will then place your chip on your selected bet space.

All The Hard Ways

For some real action when you or your date are shooting the dice, place your pass line bet down and throw. If a 'number' comes up then throw a five-dollar chip into the middle of the table and say "All the hard ways." The stickman will place four one-dollar chips on each hard way and give you one dollar change. Now you're in for some action.

When an easy way comes up on one of the hard way numbers the dealer will take away your bet. You can then toss another chip into the center and say (if, for example you lost the hard ten bet) "Hard ten back up." You can keep putting back the bets you've lost on the hard ways until you start hitting them. When you're on a hard way roll and those numbers start coming up, you will start raking in the dough, looking cool like double 0.

So play the pass line for the minimum, and the come and the hard ways when one of you is shooting.

The Special Secret Toss

Here's a craps technique that almost no one knows about, outside the dealers. And you won't find this in a gambling book either.

When people toss their chips into the center of the table for hard way, or other bets, the chips bounce and roll all over the table with the stickman chasing them around with his hands as they roll out of reach. This is sloppy and is a hassle for him.

What you can do is give the chip a counter clockwise flat spin with your fingers and wrist. When it hits the table it will stop cold right where it lands. Often you can even hit the hard way square that you call. This will even work if you throw four chips at once. Just have them stacked up in your hand and give them the same quick flat spin and they will hit the table, bounce once and stop. Cool. 007 cool.

You Finished Your Play

Okay. You've let her roll them bones. You've won a few bucks. Perhaps you gamed away a few and you're now ready to leave the table. First your stack of chips to the dealer by setting them on the table and saying "Cashing out." He will change your small chips into larger ones and push them to you on the table. Pick up your winnings and toss a five dollar chip (with a flat spin) onto the table with a "Thank you, Gentlemen." If you win more, you can tip more.

Bond's Favorite Game

"I wouldn't go banco on that."
Tracy in *OHMSS*

We often see 007 playing baccarat (Bah-ka-rah) in high-class European casinos. Baccarat was first brought to Las Vegas in The Sands hotel by Frank Sinatra to "add some class to the joint."

Baccarat is a simple card game of trying to guess which hand, the 'banker' or the 'player', will come closest to nine with two cards or an additional third card. The cool part of game is that each player gets a turn at dealing the cards out of the 'shoe'.

You can get the rules out of any gambling book and there is no skill or strategy to learn. It's simple a game of luck with the house advantage a mere 1.06 percent on the banker bet and 1.24 percent on the player bet. Thus an almost 50/50 bet. However, the usual minimum bet is twenty dollars, so you'd better enter the game with two hundred dollars.

With the best odds in the casino and the slow easy pace of the action, baccarat is a relaxing way to spend some of your casino time.

Caesars Palace casino Floor Supervisor and Vegas historian, Barney Vinsen, told me that "Less than one percent of the people that visit casinos play baccarat. So if you want to have some different gambling stories to tell when you get back home, give the game a chance, especially for you guys living the 'Bond Lifestyle'. He always plays that game, right?"

More Casino Games

I mentioned craps and the slots to entertain your girl with. But don't be afraid to learn the other games and try them out if you have a mind. The eighty casinos in Las Vegas are competing with each other so every casino is stressing courtesy. They want you to have fun and will help you with the games. Therefore don't hesitate to play a new game. Also remember to casino hop. See the varied hotel themes, shop in the malls, go on the rides and attractions and then gamble a little at different casinos.

If you start to get near the budget you made for your casino gambling be sure to take a break from the action and think about why you came to Las Vegas in the first place. Was it to gamble or enjoy your girl, family or friends? Be careful not to be such a hard core gambler that your girl gets tired of the action and is just hanging around waiting for you to finish your play. If you really have to gamble more than she wants to, do it when she is happily shopping or sleeping.

Getting Around The Strip

For getting to and from hotels and attractions in Las Vegas the best way to go is to use a taxi. The strip is usually crowded and you don't want to take the responsibility of driving when ten dollars takes you just about anywhere along the main strip. It is only fourteen dollars over to the Las Vegas Hilton to do the Star Trek attraction and twenty-two dollars to downtown's Fremont street to see the light show. Throw in a three dollar tip and you'll save time and effort, leaving you those two precious commodities to view the strip and talk to your date while the cabby (your chauffeur) gets you there. That's why there is a category for taxi money on the Mission Planner.

Taxis load conveniently at all hotels, either at the main entrance or at the side entrance. Get in the quick line, if there is one, tell the attendant where you want to go (he tells the cabby), give him a buck (most people don't, so he'll appreciate even that), get your girl safely inside and enjoy the ride.

Once you've done Las Vegas to your satisfaction, don't stop there. It's not the only Bond place in the world. Coming up are a few more.

12

MORE BOND DESTINATIONS

I'll just mention these few spots in passing and give you my short take on them. They are definitely places to consider spending some time and not just because Bond went there. You can can find additional informantion on my web site on the "00 Agents" page.

Thunderball Land

Nassau in the Bahamas can be reached by a one-hour flight out of Orlando. It's a must go place when you've got DisneyWorld on your list. This is where they shot *Thunderball* as well as the diving scenes for *20,000 Leagues Under the Sea*.

The best and most exciting hotel there is the Atlantis on Pleasure Island. This island is right next to the main island and is connected by a bridge. Gambling is permitted on Pleasure Island and the Atlantis has a great casino as well as the largest aquarium in the world that winds in, through and around the hotel and grounds.

But the real reason for going there is to take the thirty minute boat ride to Blue Lagoon island where you can swim with the dolphins for thirty minutes for a mere ninety dollars. Not just swim with them, they'll kiss you, jump over you, take a fish from your mouth, dance with you and then finally two of them will push you with their noses on your feet through the water, just like you see at the water shows. Only you're the show. You do this with a life preserver on, and under the trainer's supervision. So it's completely safe and the water temperature is just perfect.

There is also a program where you go in the water waist deep and touch the dolphins, which is great for younger, older and apprehensive visitors. This is not to be missed in this lifetime.

Live and Let Die Land

New Orleans has been in that Bond movie (and others too numerous to mention). Be sure to stay in the French Quarter to soak up the atmosphere. There is a Harrah's casino there if you feel the urge. Mostly it's the atmosphere of 'the quarter' that gives you the fun. Be sure to take a three hour Mississippi paddleboat tour with the jazz band playing and the swamp tour to go alligator hunting.

A View To A Kill Land

San Francisco has got to be the most beautiful city in the world with its forty-two hills, the largest Chinatown outside of Hong Kong, Fisherman's Wharf and that wonderful Golden Gate Bridge in the fog.

Be sure to stay only at Fisherman's Wharf. That's

where all the action is. Right outside your door will be tours, Ghiradelli Square, the Cannery, Alcatraz Island, Pier 39 and the Bay Cruise boats. The Holiday Inn at Fisherman's Wharf and the Sheraton right next to Pier 39 are the two best hotels.

Other excursions leave from there which include the Napa/Sonoma wine country tour, the Monterey/Carmel tour, Santa Cruz and the 'roaring camp' railroad tour. One that takes you further down the coast is the Hearst Castle tour.

You can even fly or take a train (thirteen hours round trip) to Yosemite Valley. As you are in San Francisco, the three hour tour of the city is a must. After that you can get around the small city on your own with bus, taxi and cable car.

Be *The Man with the Golden Gun*

Phuket Island is where Scaramonga had his hideaway in that Bond film. It's just off the coast of Thailand. I spent fifteen days there, as I told you, and it's just heaven, even more than Hawaii. There are many wonderful beach resorts there so you'll have to read up on them at my site and choose one for yourself.

Be sure to take an overnight excursion to Pi Pi Island (pronounced pee pee), which is about a three hour boat ride. It's a small island with just one hotel and it will make you feel like you just got off The Bounty with Fletcher Christian. Yes, that was Tahiti, but this place is the spitting image of it.

The World Is Not Enough

It is, however, a good place to start. See and enjoy the places you're curious about. Study up on the cultures that you are visiting so you can really get the feel of the country you're in. Most of all - enjoy!

Never Take a Vacation

The idea of 'taking a vacation' sounds like you are doing something outside your life. Something that you don't do often. Possibly with the feeling of 'escaping' your job or aparment.

Your vacation should be thought of as an extension of your life, not something seperate. When it's time to return home and to your job, this should be a happy experience as well. A new beginning. Not the end of a vacation. Not the end of good times.

So keep up that vacation freedom and energy when you return home. If you like you can turn your apartment into an extension of your favorite hotel by purchasing items like that hotel's towels, soap, shampoo and other symbols to keep you in that vacation feeling at home. This way, no matter at home or on a vacation you are always living the James Bond lifestyle.

13

VILLAINS

Who's your favorite villain in the Bond movies? Mine is Donald Grant in *From Russia with Love*. I love the line he says on the train where he's holding a gun on 007. Bond is on his knees forced to keep his hands in his pockets and Grant is sitting on the sofa arm with his foot on the sofa. "The first one won't kill you," Grant says referring to the bullets in his gun. "Nor the second. Not even the third. Not till you crawl over here and KISS MY FOOT."

Villains are entertaining in the Bond movies, but in real life they are a different thing. Let's discuss the various types of villains that you will encounter.

"Gate crasher. I'll leave you to clean up."
Bond to knocked out villain in *OHMSS*

Having put on a lot of events, parties and movie productions, 'gate crashers' are a pet peeve of mine. These are people who come to your event and make trouble. It's easy for them because they didn't put any time, effort or money into the event. When they don't have an investment in your event they don't have respect for it either. They come to get what entertainment value that they can from it and then head off looking for another event to crash. Their behavior may range from simple loud obnoxious talking to starting fights. Usually it's in the range of them complaining about what a crappy event you're having and why isn't there more food or girls.

The problem with gate crashers is that you never see them coming. Naturally, if they did it to you once you wouldn't invite them again or even let them know of your event. Unfortunately it seems like each new event draws out another couple of new gate crashers.

Having done many martial arts events and movies, security was never a problem because everyone there was a black belt in karate or kung fu. No, the problem would be like this true story:

I hired a young kung fu teacher and his group of six students to do some martial arts fights in a large-scale action scene I was directing on a horse ranch. I had permission from the ranch owner who gave me explicit instructions to always have the gate closed after our cars drove in to keep the horses from getting out.

Everything was going well for the day as I went from filming dialogue scenes to a large action scene with my star, Eric Lee, fighting many villains on the run with his double swords. Between camera set ups, this kung fu teacher I mentioned comes up to me and says, "We want to kill Eric Lee."

"What do you mean?" I asked.

"We want to kill him in this scene."

"But in this scene Eric wins the battle. He's the hero."

"But our kung fu techniques are better than Eric's so we should kill him."

I couldn't believe what I was hearing and proceeded blindly into this idiotic conversation with a guy that was hired and paid to be a martial arts fighting extra. Here he was, an extra, saying that he wanted to rewrite the movie and kill the hero. "Well" I said, trying to be polite, "Eric is the star of the movie and the script says that he wins this battle."

"But we could kill him because our martial arts skills are better than his." He repeated his outrageous reasoning.

I tried a new way of addressing the problem to get this guy out of my hair and me back to work. "Well, Eric is the producer of this movie" I lied, "so he wants to be the hero and live."

"Then I'm taking my men and leaving" he threatened.

This was music to my ears because I had about forty martial artists that day and didn't need his six. "Well, okay" I said, trying to sound disappointed. "I guess it can't be helped. But I appreciate the scenes that you did today. They looked good. I'll tell you when we have the premier."

"Fine," he said. In a huff he turned with his men to leave.

Then I said a stupid thing that I still regret. "Be sure to close the gate on your way out."

Well, you can guess the rest of the story. He purposely left the gate open, the horses got out onto the road, the owner had to go round them up and then he kicked us off his ranch. I could only apologize to the owner and get the cast and crew out. Who could argue with him after the dangerous situation that had occurred where his precious horses were mixing with traffic?

Maybe even if I hadn't said it, that Clyde would still have left the gate open or done something else strange. Thank God, I found another and even better location to do those scenes.

Anyway, it was very easy for this guy to cause trouble since he had no investment in the movie, a movie that took me two years to finance and was very risky. The production was put in greater jeopardy because of this kung fu teacher who was literally a 'gate crasher.'

You know, thinking back, I can remember that at the audition for fighting extras, that same kung fu teacher asked to talk to me privately. When I took the time to talk with him he started going on and on about how he wanted to "show his art for the camera". I said "Sure, the camera will pick up your fighting techniques clearly because we're filming in Panavision." Just the fact that he wanted to speak to me privately, when the others were content to audition and leave, should have been some kind of warning to me that he was a possible trouble maker.

All I can advise you to do is keep your eyes and ears open to this kind of person. If there are any strange words or actions coming from someone you might deem as a possible gate crasher, keep him away from your event. Remember these Clydes like to be invited, giving them mental free rein to do whatever they please once they arrive at your event. It makes me think of the old vampire lore that states: "A vampire is powerless to enter a home unless the man of the house invites him in." I think the same folklore holds true for the devil. You have to invite him in. As much as we don't want to admit it, most of the villains that have plagued us in the past, we have invited into our homes, parties, events and lives. Be careful whom you invite.

Comedian Jerry Lewis said in a serious interview, "If someone comes into your house and the baby starts crying and the dog runs and hides, you'd better get that guy out of your house as soon as possible."

Time Wasters

Now that you have set out to live like 007, time wasters are easy to spot and easy to take care of. Just remember that there are some people that you'd like to spend hours with, but not days. Some people you'd like to spend minutes with, but not hours. There are some people that don't even qualify for minutes of your precious time. Time that you could use to move forward on your goals. Time just to be alone and think.

While you're thinking, ask yourself this: "What have my friends got me doing, got me reading, got me thinking? And is that good for me or not?"

If you're hanging around time wasters, it's your fault not theirs. To rephrase an old adage, "Waste my time once, a curse on you. Waste my time twice, a curse on me."

Eternal 'No Action' Students

Once you start to upgrade your life people are going to notice it. You will be excited about your new approach to life and want everyone to experience the adventure and excitement of taking control of their lives and changing their dreams into real experiences. Thus, there will be those that will be inspired to take action along with you and those that just want your attention with no intention of their own to move forward. They will want constant meetings with you so that you can tell them everything that you're doing and give them advice for their problems, not goals mind you, but their problems. They will bend your ears and use you like a free psychiatrist, dumping all their negativity and complaints about people in their lives onto you. This is the reason why psychiatrists have a high suicide rate. They take in too much negativity. Well, that is their chosen profession and they are well paid for it. But if you're not being well compensated for it, then it's best to recommend a professional counselor for your complacent friend.

On the other hand, if a friend starts using the advice you give him, even coming back for more and taking action on that too, he will be a good ally for you and even inspire you.

If you deem your friend to be an 'eternal student' who just wants your time and attention, give him a copy of this book and tell him 'this is all you need to get started.' Then waste no further time with him.

You Teach People How to Treat You

That's right. All these years you have taught people how to respect or not respect you, your time, your home, your personal items and your car. If you don't like the way they're doing that, then it's time to gently re-educate them. Remember that it's not their fault that they treat you like that. It was you who taught them to be that way to you. Every time they dropped by unannounced and helped themselves to everything in your refrigerator, grabbed books and videos off of your shelf to take home without asking or borrowed your car without replacing the gas, and you said nothing about it, you were teaching them.

This is another example of how everything in your life good or bad has been attracted or created by you. Once again, don't blame them; don't even blame yourself. Just take the responsibility to re-educate them. If they don't like the idea that you are no longer a door mat for them to wipe their feet on, if they say "You've changed," you don't have to make a speech. Merely say "I have a lot of new things that I have to do and my schedule is very full now, so I've had to re-orient my daily lifestyle."

If, for example, you've told friends not to drop by unless they call first and they still knock on your door, you have every right not to answer it. Otherwise, remind them that you have asked them to call first and you are in the middle of some important business, so you can't accept visitors at time. Now that you are taking important action in your life, that statement will be true. You will always have important business to do. You'll either be planning, doing or taking a break from attending to your goals. You might be studying or reading an important book or listening to a tape course. You might be programming your mind by watching a Bond video. Whatever it is, that is what you decided to do with your time and not take in an unannounced time waster. Besides, your real friends will respect your time and always call.

This is only one example of how you will have to gently re-educate people in your circle of influence so that you'll be treated the way you want.

Richard Burton vs. Six Villains

When actor Richard Burton was in his thirties he and a friend were walking down the streets of London at night when six street punks made some snide remarks at him. He immediately dove into the group and started fighting. The youths got him on the ground and kicked him numerous times in the back and then ran off.

After that he always had back pains. Think about it. All the time he was making those movies, married to Elizabeth Taylor, vacationing in Puerto Vallarta and traveling the world, he had back pains (which may have accelerated his drinking). All this because he had to take on some Clydes whose only claim to fame is that they once beat up Richard Burton.

Fellow Bond fan, it's not worth getting into altercations with low vibrational people. You and I both know that there are low life people these days carrying pistols under their jackets that will pull them out and use them for no other reason than the wrong look. So you'll have to make the intellectual decision right now to let those predators go by. Not to be angered by them when they stare you down or say some bad remark. The only important thing for you to do is get yourself and your loved ones out of there and safely home.

Your loved ones should not have to spend the rest of their lives in court trying to get justice for your death. They should spend the rest of their lives having you take them to all kinds of exciting places. Having you guide and encouraging them into exciting lifestyles. Not mourning the anniversary of your demise by some scum. Besides, if you had killed him, you'd be in prison, but he may only get five years probation for killing you.

One way to look at it is, if he challenges you to a fight, it's not a fair fight because you have an exciting lifestyle, apartment, job, friends, money and dreams. If you go to prison or die, you lose that. If he goes to prison or dies, what does he give up? A couple of beers a night while riding around in his gang's beat up car. That's all. Let him first accumulate the success you have and then he can risk that when he wants to fight. Then, maybe it's a fair fight.

Those are the thoughts to have, but keep them to yourself and stay away. I've often heard people on TV say "That bad man was wrong to kill that nice guy." Well, yes he was. He was a predator. Just like the lion in the jungle. So you should have respect for his wild unpredictable actions and stay the hell away from all predators.

My karate teacher once said: "Even if you win a fight, you get your clothes torn, body scratched and evening ruined. So it's not worth it." He also said: "If you fight a knife man, you have to chose where you want the knife to go, in your arm or in your stomach. So it's not worth it."

'Don't Do That'

Probably the greatest villains are the ones that talk people out of their dreams. Because the person who was talked out of taking action will live out his lifetime without even getting a piece of that dream. Without even seeing a glimpse of that dream. All because at a pivotal point in his life he listened to a friend who said: "Don't go to college, don't date that girl, don't go to Las Vegas, don't write a book, don't do a second Bond movie (as George Lazenby was advised). Let's have a couple of beers and watch reruns of *Gilligan's Island*."

If you listen to that kind of advice, you'll end up on *Gilligan's Island*, but not with the beautiful Tina Louise. You'll end up making coconut telephones with your friend Clyde and a six pack.

Don't let anyone talk you out of your dreams.

BOND INTERACTS WITH PEOPLE

"I want to meet him socially."
Bond in *Dr. No*

Part of Bond's allure is that he often operates alone. However, don't make the mistake of believing that being a loner is the way to go. Social interaction is an important and satisfying part of life. I've seen too many people in the entertainment world harboring secret fantasies about making it big and then dumping the people that they are clinging to desperately for support – until they make it. I've seen a couple of people in my group of filmmakers who have done that very thing, then came crawling back to the people that they dumped once they ran out of luck getting jobs. Needless to say, they weren't welcomed back. Worse, they didn't make any new friends while they were hot. So they ended up alone, lacking the social skills to start up a new circle of friends. They finally got stuck with other social misfits just like themselves who weren't very entertaining and merely sufficed as boredom killers.

When an interviewer asked Wally 'Famous' Amos what it was like to be completely independent, he answered "I can't be completely independent. I need people to make my cookies and I need people to buy my cookies."

Even the self-reliant Bond needed help turning off the atomic time bomb in *Goldfinger*.

Movie Note: In *Goldfinger*, that sequence was originally filmed with the bomb being turned off with the counter reading "003," indicating three seconds remaining. However, the producer got the good idea during editing to have it stop at "007." This was cut into the film and always got a great laugh and release of tension in the theaters. However, Bond's line remained the same, "Three more clicks and Mr. Goldfinger would have hit the jackpot."

"I'm so lonely. What can I do?"

An old man called a friend of mine and started crying on the phone about how lonely he was. My friend, who was his nephew, sent his two children over to his house to stay a couple of days to cheer him up. When I first heard that story I felt sad for the guy. But now years later, I'm wondering why this man didn't cultivate friends before it came to that. Or why he didn't take action on getting some friends. Maybe he wasn't a giver. To get friends and keep them you have to give.

Think about it. There are children in everybody's neighborhood that would love to be taken to the movies, amusement park or the circus. There are parents who would love someone to take their kids there. I call this 'rent-a-kid'. When I was a child my father's friend, Ralph, used to pick me up and take me to the carnival once or twice a year. Ralph had no kids of his own and loved going to the carnival so he 'rented' me for a few hours and took me there. We became great friends all through his life.

It's time to think about making friends to go through life with. You can do this at any time, at any age. Just invite someone to the movies, or rent some neighbor kids and take them to the circus.

Be Early

I've never seen Bond running out the door yelling, "I'm late. I'll never make it." He seems to always be on time. This is an important reputation to have. In fact, early is better, except for a home or office appointment. In those cases, exactly on time is best. Don't arrive before they are ready to receive you.

However, in the case of meeting someone outside, in front of a theater, bus stop or restaurant for example, early is best. When you are early it speaks a lot about you to other people. When you are early you are saying: "I am organized. I know what I'm doing. I respect your time as well as my time."

When you're late, you are also communicating many things to the people waiting for you. Things like: "I don't know what I'm doing. I'm confused. I don't plan ahead. I have no respect for people's time or my own."

Nancy Sinatra said of her father, "He always allowed enough time to shower, shave, get dressed and take care of final grooming, like shining his shoes and removing lint from his jacket before going out. And he always arrived 10 minutes early to where he was going, be it a business appointment or social."

Develop the reputation of being early, especially when meeting your Bond girl. She'll really appreciate it. Think about her coming to the meeting place and wondering if you'll be there or not. There you will be - relaxed and prepared for the fun at hand. Now that's very Bond.

However, don't fall into the trap of arriving early and then killing time by dropping into a bookstore or restroom. If the person that you are meeting arrives a little early, then you've missed your big chance to be there waiting for them and all your efforts to arrive early will have been wasted.

Say to yourself: "Okay, I got here early and I'm going to wait here and get the credit for arriving early. Later I'll hit the restroom or bookstore, once I establish contact with the person I'm waiting for."

Why Should We Visit Bond At His Home?

Because it's a happening place. Bond will tell us all kinds of exciting stories. If he's home at all, that is. If he is, he'll probably have some interesting people visiting him there, if not some charming woman. Yes, let's give Bond a call and see if we can drop by. I can't wait to talk to him. How about you?

Now! Why should anyone drop by your place? Is it a happening place? Do you have interesting stories? Are you about to go on a mission? Are you just coming back from one? Have encouraging things to tell your guest? Is your refrigerator stocked with food for your guests?

I've noticed that in my early twenties I had lots of college buddies to call on and visit. After age twenty-seven, just being a college friend wasn't enough reason to see them. They had to be happening, interesting and productive. Otherwise it was more important and interesting to work on my projects.

For this reason, you should always have a project that you're working on to tell people about, so that you have something to answer besides, "Nothing much," when they greet you with "What's new?"

"I hope you'll forgive me, but it's most important,"
Bond excusing himself from the baccarat table in *Dr. No*

Common courtesy shows strength of character, charm and breeding. Real courtesy comes from the heart. You don't have to read a book on manners. You don't have to stand anymore when a lady enters the room or leaves the table. But a few well chosen sincere words at the right time, as in a well timed compliment, shows more class then a well cut tuxedo.

Keep your eyes open for opportunities to give a compliment. Flattery is easy. But to catch the person in the act of doing something well, takes talent. And it takes even more talent to search out and select just the right words to convey your appreciation for what they did, gave or accomplished.

Your Word Is Your Bond

Picture yourself talking on the phone with your friend. In that conversation you happen to mention a video you haven't seen. Your friend casually says, "Oh, I have a copy of that. I'll send it to you." You say, "Great. I'll look forward to it. Thanks." Then you continue with the conversation.

For the next week you check your mailbox. What happens? That's right. Your friend never sent you that video.

Sounds familiar doesn't it? Now, your friend is a good person. He means well, but he seldom, if ever, follows up on his promises. It was a casual promise made on something that was not so important, like that video, so there's no harm done. You could go to the video shop and rent it yourself. And after all everybody's like that.

What happens the next time that person says he'll send you something? You may say to him, "Right. Great. Thank you." But you say to yourself, "It will never be sent. It will be forgotten by him before this conversation is over."

Now it's important to ask yourself, if James Bond said he'd send you a MI-6 attaché case, or his spare tuxedo, or his extra laser watch, would you find it in the mail that week? No, you wouldn't. It would be sent to your door by express delivery service that same day with a note that reads, "I hope you enjoy this. Nice talking with you." Signed James Bond.

Now ask yourself, whose reputation do you want to have? Your friend's reputation? The one who never keeps his word? Or Bond's reputation? Whose word is his bond?

Keeping your word can be a little hectic. Because if you make a lot of promises you'll be too busy carrying all of them out to have anytime left over for yourself. Be careful of the promises you make. But do carry out all promises. Even the small ones, or especially the small ones, because ninety percent of the things you promise will be the small things.

So protect your reputation and your word.

Tightwads From Hell

You never want to get the reputation of being cheap. One thing about cheap people is that they never get that reputation mistakenly. If someone is called cheap, believe me, he is cheap. I'm only speaking about people with ample money, who hold on to it and always let others pay for them. If you already have that reputation, start changing it – or you're going to end up on people's list of tightwads. Here are a couple of them that I know of personally.

My Dad went out to lunch with a couple of his long time friends. When it came time to pay the bill, his rich friend Fred said, "Oh, sorry I forgot my wallet. I'll get it next time." After they paid the bill and Fred drove off, my Dad's other friend said, "Have you noticed that every time we go to lunch with Fred he always forgets his wallet?" "Yeah," my Dad replied. "And come to think of it, he's forgotten his wallet every time for the last twenty years."

One distant relative of mine has a trick that he uses when he has lunch with people. When the bill comes and everyone is throwing their money in the middle of the table, he pulls out a fifty dollar bill and holds it tight between both hands, waiting for someone to say, "That's okay, hold on to your fifty. I've got it." Happily for him, someone always does. He's probably had that same fifty-dollar bill for fifty years.

Another guy I know, who never takes his wife out was finally pushed to take her to Reno for some gambling. He wouldn't gamble, so does he leaves her alone to have some fun on the slot machines? No. He leans his elbow on the machine next to her, puts his head on his hand, and watches her the whole time, following her around the casino from machine to machine. He is a combination tightwad and party pooper. Out of boredom, he took two quarters out of his wife's money tray and put them in the machine he was leaning on and won a $200 jackpot. What did he do with the $200? Well, we've got to give him credit for giving the jackpot to his wife.

Millionaire tightwads are in a category of their own with deep psychological problems. Not being able to even take their wives out to dinner for fear of parting with their 'hard earned' money. Many go to counseling to gradually learn how let go of a few bucks so they can take their wives to a few restaurants and weekend trips to avoid divorce. So when you hit the millionaire mark, be sure to circulate a little cash so as to have fun and be fun.

Don't Be A Wet Blanket

Make sure to join in on any activity that you go to. Get into the experience, even though it may not be your particular interest. For example, if you don't drink, yet end up touring a winery and tasting room, you can pick up one glass of wine and take a small sip and say something about it. Or look around the gift shop and buy a few postcards or a bottle of wine for a gift. At least pretend that you're into the experience. Just don't stand there with a 'when will this be over?' expression on your face.

Remember, when you see an old guy wet blanket at an event, he probably started out as a young guy wet blanket and never took the energy to change. He's now probably blaming his age as the reason for him being unpopular.

Exploding Hand Grenade

Once I heard a man say, "I love my wife and son so much I would do anything for them. I would hold a hand grenade on my chest, and let it explode for them." A couple of days later, his twelve-year-old son asked him for a ride to the movie theater. His father replied, "Ah, why don't you just take the bus."

Well, I guess driving his son to the movie theater didn't fall into the category of exploding hand grenades.

So when you tell yourself that you'd do anything for your family or girlfriend, ask yourself if you would drive them to a movie theater or take them to the dentist. These are the things that are usually needed. Having to explode a hand grenade on your chest rarely comes up.

New Relationships

Whether it's a new business or new personal relationship,

your image and reputation will be carved in granite with your first actions. So be very sure to show up early for those first meetings. To have your cash ready when it comes time to chip in for those first restaurant bills. To do what you promised. To dress the way you want to be thought of. Because after four or five meetings, your image is set.

If later on down the line you happen to be late or forget to do something, that person won't think too much about it because this is not the norm for you. Just remember not to make a new pattern of that error. Be early on the next appointment and fulfill your next promise perfectly and on time, so as to re-establish your prior reputation.

Never Say These Words Again

"I'm busy." Did you ever invite someone to go someplace and their simple answer was, "I'm busy." How did you feel? Probably the person who said it didn't realize it, but "I'm busy" is a double insult. First he is insinuating that you are not busy. Second, it sounds like "My life is more important than what you are inviting me to do."

If you can't accept someone's invitation, it's best to avoid the easy and common "I'm busy" and use a longer explanation of why you can't go. Something along the lines of, "I'd really like to, but I have a business appointment on that day."

The words "I'll try" should also be eliminated from your list of expressions. "I'll try" hints at not wanting to take on the responsibility of a commitment to the invitation. It also has the meaning of 'If nothing comes up better for me that day then maybe I'll come to your event.' It's best to commit to going at that time or to say that you're already booked during the time of event.

"I'm busy" and "I'll try" are now gone from your expression list. It'll take a few times to break the habit, but it can be done and will set you apart from the crowd socially as well as in business.

Instead of using the word 'busy' when someone asks you how your day was, say "I had a productive day. I accomplished a lot." Now there is a powerful statement with positive images. Everybody has a busy day, but did they accomplish anything? Using the word 'accomplish' shows that you've successfully finished tasks. Using the word 'productive' also shows completed work. They're much stronger images then the standard "I had a busy day."

A Lesson From *Mad* Magazine

In high school, I saw a cartoon in *Mad* magazine that had only five frames to it. The first frame showed a boss yelling at his worker. The next frame showed the worker at home yelling at his wife. Next was the wife yelling at her son. Then her son yelling at his younger brother. Finally the brother was shown yelling at the family dog.

Passing down a bad experience to someone lower on the totem pole seemed ridiculous to me. I remember making a decision while looking at that chain of events in the magazine that I would never become a comic link by passing down someone's anger to my friends or family. I would refuse to participate in that yelling chain.

Included in that would be passing down a bad remark that someone said about someone else, as in "Do you know what he said about you?" I refuse to be some negative Clyde's messenger service. That's why later on you will see as one of the Bond lifestyle rules, "I circulate all things good. The bad stops with me."

Correspondence

"You are not even important enough for me to take the 15 seconds to hit the reply button and write one line. I don't want to hear from you again, so I am ignoring your email and you altogether."

Does that sound harsh to you? That's what you are saying when you don't reply to someone's email. In the days when there was only regular mail, it took a lot of effort to write, address, stamp and get a letter to the post box. But email is different. Hit the reply button and send a short note like, "Hi James, Thanks for the email. My schedule's really full right now. I'll write you again soon." It's very easy and can be done in a few seconds, even if your house is on fire.

I've often heard it discussed how someone hasn't returned an email in weeks, leaving the one who is waiting for a response to wonder what is going on with that relationship. The excuse of "I've been busy" doesn't hold up anymore with email.

If you want to cut a relationship with the person, that's fine. You can even put an address block on him. If you want to maintain it, then answer him within a few days, at least.

By all means, if someone sends you a gift, be sure to get out a thank you email, letter or a phone call to let them know that you received and appreciate it. Yeah, just like when your mother told you to write your aunt for sending you that toy. Only now, you're an adult with more serious relationships at stake. (Not to demean your aunt.)

Connecting To People

Remember that even though you will have to go it alone most of the time in your quest for living the James

Bond lifestyle, always build your relationships with the people of your choice. It's only when connecting with people that we are truly alive.

15

BOND ON THE JOB

"Her Majesty's secret service is still my job."
Bond to Tracy in *OHMSS*

I'm often asked, "Where do I get the money if I want to start this Bond lifestyle?" My answer is simple: "From your job." Bond is a working man. He has a government salaried position. If you want to live his lifestyle you have to keep working. The most important thing that should come from your job is money. Satisfaction should come from your lifestyle. If you can get some kind of satisfaction from your job, as in being efficient, accomplishing things and helping your company make a profit, then that's fine. But first do it for the cash. Cash to use to get your piece of the Bond lifestyle.

Don't Kill The Golden Goose

Don't risk your job or quit your job in the name of starting a new lifestyle. Use those monthly golden eggs to finance your upgraded existence and then search for another job if you're ready to move up. I've seen many people purposefully put a knife into their own goose. No more golden eggs, just cooked goose.

I guess the reason for this is that success is harder than failure. You've heard about that before and maybe, like me, you can't understand why that would be. But if you think about it, success means responsibility, action, decisions, schedules and commitment. Failure means getting up any time of the day and watching whatever rerun of *Gomer Pile* happens to be on. That's easy.

The hard working pop singer Madonna, who's always working on a project said, "I wanted to be rich and famous so that I wouldn't have any more problems. Now I have more problems than before." This should not be a reason for you to quit your goal. Just a realization of what happens when you get there.

Arnold Shwartzenegger said, "Once you reach the top you have to always work to keep your value up, like a rare stamp."

Sinatra's Biggest Enemy

When Sinatra was thirty-four his career was virtually over. He lost his voice, his MGM acting contract, his recording contract and his MCA agents dropped him. A few years later he got back on his feet with an academy award for his supporting role in *From Here to Eternity*. He then got serious and built an empire of film productions, recordings, nightclub performances and casino hotels.

When he was asked the reason for his earlier failure he answered, "Me. I was the reason. I'm my own worst enemy. It happened because I paid no attention to how I was singing. Instead, I wanted to sit back, enjoy my success and sign autographs. Well, let me tell you that nobody who is successful sits back and enjoys it. I learned that the hard way. You work at it all the time, even harder than when you were a nobody. Enjoyment is just a byproduct. If you get a kick out of it, fine. But the real fun of success is working hard at the thing that brought you success. That's what I had to learn. You hear all the time about guys who showed big promise or who even made it to the top and then suddenly they flub out. Everybody says they must have developed a block or lost their touch or one of the guys at the office was out to get them or whatever. Well, maybe that's just a fancy way of saying the thing I found out: The only guy that can hurt you is you yourself."

Your Most Important Job Skill

To be successful at your job, you have to get along with people. In fact, job researchers have said that your job skill is only twenty percent of your reason for success at work. Eighty percent of job success is attributed to your people skills. How you interact with your co-workers and boss. This makes sense to me. In fact, after hiring numerous actors and crewmembers on my movies and working with them, I can tell you the reason that they are rehired is for their ability to work efficiently with others. The complainers, troublemakers and loafers are not asked back. There's too much at stake and too much time lost having to deal with their problems.

Just ask yourself, what kind of worker would you want at your company or on your project? Would you hire yourself on a particular job or project?

Always Be A Professional

A professional, of course, is someone who gets paid for a certain type of work. But 'being professional' means performing your job well, no matter what you are feeling at the moment about the situation, the people you're working with or your own personal problems. You are there to get the job done, period. Having the reputation of being professional will be a big plus for your advancement in the company or searching for another job.

Expand Beyond Your Job Description

The expression, "It's not my job" should never be one of yours. If someone needs something done that's not in your area or job description, then take him to someone who can help him or take care of it yourself, as long as it doesn't encroach on anyone else's territory. Generally speaking, if you more than fill your job area, it will help you advance.

My friend, Bob, started working at Warner Brothers Studio as an assistant running the studio's transportation department. The boss of that department liked to take it easy so he told Bob to take over as much responsibility as he wanted. Bob answered all the phone calls and took care of everyone's requests. Soon everyone thought Bob was running the department. After handling one director's requests frequently, the director asked Bob if he wanted to be an assistant director for him. That was the opportunity that he was waiting for and quickly moved up to working with that director on the TV series *Fantasy Island*. All because Bob expanded beyond his job description and did more than he was contracted to do.

Remember Q in the movie *Octopussy*? He exceeded his job description to go on a raid with Bond. Do you remember Q's reward for it? That's right. Girls, girls, girls.

Help The Customer First

Jack LaLane started a chain of health clubs and his number one advice for his managers was to push the customers to have a hard work out for at least twenty minutes. "Have them do a hard workout before they hit the sauna and Jacuzzi. This way they will feel stronger and get stronger every week and continue to come back. Help the customer first, and the money will come."

This seems to be the most important thing to concentrate on. But it's often forgotten. In business financial considerations prevail, but your ultimate satisfaction should come from helping your customers.

Bond Has Respect For M

Think about that one. Everyone has a boss. Bond is his own man, but has to stay in line when he's in M's presence. That's because it's up to M to send Bond on the good missions or not and to give him the back up of MI-6 and Q Branch. Ultimately, M approves Bond's paycheck. Without a good working relationship there would be no paycheck, no luxury resort hotels, no golf, no gas for his car and soon no car.

As recent history shows, even the President of the United States, the most powerful man in the world, has a boss: the American people. If he rocks the boat too much or plays too much grab ass on that boat, the people are going to put him in line.

Remember all this when your boss gets a little too demanding or gruff with you. He's just another M. And if you are not comfortable with him, like having your hand in extremely hot or cold water that doesn't match your hand's vibrational rate, then make plans and take strategic action to get yourself to a higher vibrational job with a higher vibrational boss. As far as this goes, usually negotiating a department switch will do the trick.

"I'm bored at my job."

You're bored at work? That's actually good. Boredom is a type of pain, and pain for a short time is good. This is your higher intelligence telling you to move up to a higher vibrational experience.

Now, your first reaction will be to 'escape' from your job. Escape conjures up the image of a prison, and a prison is a hard thing to escape from. Better to move your mental, emotional and even physical vibrations higher and float out of your lower vibrational job, like a helium filled balloon naturally seeking its own vibrational level.

You can raise your vibrations by not hating your boss or co-workers, by refusing to fight or compete with them, and by studying something to raise your mental vibration, thereby raising your value in the market place. You can also put energy into job searching.

The next time you're feeling bored at your job (or any place for that matter), thank your higher intelligence for the message. If there is stronger mental and emotional pain, take that as a warning to float out of that situation quickly.

While we're on the subject, never verbalize your boredom. Saying I'm bored is like saying, "Hey world, come entertain me." If you say "I'm bored," especially in this modern society of vast entertainment, you are in effect saying, "I'm a boring person."

So make note here, boredom and pain are warnings telling you to move out of that experience. If there were no such thing as boredom or pain, all of us would be satisfied with the same TV dinner and the same episode of *Leave it to Beaver*.

This is why variety, along with survival, to feel important and to love and be loved, is one of the four basic human needs.

Bored at the job? Take action.

Be In The Top Ten Percent

It has been reported that within a thirty-day period only fifty percent of workers show up at work every day. Some get sick and some take days off. Only twenty percent show up on time every day in that same thirty-day period. Only ten percent show up, on time, ready to work. Others have to hit the coffee machine, the rest room or gab with other workers. So if you show up, on time, ready to work, you'll be in the top ten percent.

This reminds me of when I was filming *Omega Cop* and the make-up girl kept coming in later every day. Make-up is needed first thing for the actors, so it was important that she be there on time. Finally a few nights before we finished, she showed up an hour late carrying a pizza for her friends on the crew. I turned to my assistant and said, "Well, she showed up... late... ready to eat. I guess one out of three isn't too bad. We should at least be thankful that she showed up at all."

Your Secret Weapon in Business

On one of the movies I was directing, I needed a high fall from a stuntman in a scene where one of the major characters dies. The regular fee for a very high fall off a cliff would have been $10,000. A stunt man who I had befriended said he'd do if for $3000. This was a great bargain and would help make the movie look bigger budget than it was. However, the producer didn't want to pay more than

$2000, so the stunt was to be changed to a smaller fall.

I tried to reason this out with the producer, but to no avail. Knowing that this was a special scene in an important movie for me, I used my newly invented secret weapon. I told the stunt man to lie and say he would do the stunt for the $2000, and then I secretly paid him the extra $1000 out of my own pocket. To this day the producer still doesn't know about it.

The name of this secret weapon is: Use your own money.

Sometimes in business when the company doesn't want to pay for an expense that would move a project forward or ease the execution of your job, use your secret weapon. Most importantly, don't tell anyone. If you reveal that you intend to pay for it yourself, you are becoming combative and prideful; challenging the company, which could be detrimental to you. So if you need to take a special client out to dinner or gift him, or need to get a hotel room or use a taxi that the company won't authorize, and you feel that it is important for you to get the job done in a proper manner, then use your secret weapon. Use your own cash. Be sure that you only use it when you deem it absolutely necessary. When it is, use it.

Just knowing that you have the use of this secret weapon will free up your thinking and help your job performance, whether you are forced to use it or not.

That great high fall stunt that I paid for years ago is still in the movie where new friends see it. It also has a special camera and editing technique that hadn't been previously used in American movies at that time, so I got to enjoy using and showing that innovation. Since then I have earned back the $1000 dollars many times over. But that was the time to get that shot. Not now when the filming is long over.

An MI-6 Agent vs. Freelance Operator

Though Bond is for Her Majesty all the way, he is also a freelance. When he's in the field, it's up to him to survive. He knows that if MI-6 loses its funding, then he's out of a job fast. He knows that in truth everybody is a freelance. America used to have forty years guaranteed employment for their workers. So did Japan. That has changed completely in America and is changing fast in Japan.

Don't forget that you are a freelance. Do a great job at the company, but do a better job on yourself. Expand those skills that you can sell in the market place. Expand your network of business contacts. Have some survival money stored away or at least some gold sovereigns. Because your company could fold tomorrow. If it does, you won't. Right?

Paid To Be Bond

Being a freelance all my life, I've always marveled at the idea of having a paid vacation. Though I've had some wonderful 'working vacations' I think that when someone goes on a vacation and comes back to a company paycheck waiting for them, they have a lot to be thankful for. They get to plan a Bond-like trip and then come back to the cash that can pay for it. All I'm saying here is to be sure to not take your paid vacation for granted. Enjoy it.

Those of you that are freelance and can go away for six weeks of fun, don't come back as one guy did who called me and said, "I'm in credit card hell."

Don't take the trip if you can't pay the tip. Be responsible for the choice you made. Come back and show your friends the photos. But the trip was your responsibility, so don't complain about the debt you're in. Besides, it's bad for your image, your prosperity thinking and bad for your friendships.

And for Bond's sake, don't tell the girl that you took that you're in "credit card hell." Just do what everyone does from Bond to Sinatra; roll up your sleeves, get to work and silently pay off the debts you incurred while having fun.

As I said earlier, I choose my trips and expenditures well, so that when I come back from a trip, I'm in 'credit card heaven.'

Before You Quit Your Job

Speaking of those plastic passports of compounding interest, if you are contemplating quitting or changing your job, be sure to call your credit card companies and have them raise your credit limits a couple of thousand dollars. They'll do it if you're still working. It's harder when you're not. Don't worry about the temptation of the extra credit, you're wise enough to know if, when and what to use it on. Furthermore, "It's better to have credit and not need it than to...." Well, you know the chant.

The only company that I was ever on salary for was Paramount Studios for three months. At that time I got two more credit cards and added credit to my other two. Thank God I took that action because those cards sustained me through a dry spell that came later.

Good Luck In Business

Frank Sinatra said, "Luck is only important insofar as getting the chance to sell yourself at the right moment. After that, you've got to have talent and know how to use it."

A saying about luck that I like is: "Luck is where opportunity meets preparation." This echoes Sinatra's words, but might be a more helpful slogan because a person's talent must be nurtured with hard work. That's why 'preparation' is needed.

Actor Charles Grodin let his chance for starring in *The Graduate* get fouled up by asking for more money than was offered. He was not given his next opportunity for three years. He said, "I didn't have a job, so while waiting all I could do was study my acting and get better." He finally got his big break in *The Heartbreak Kid*.

Make An Atom Bomb

Years ago I had a frustrating wait trying to get my third feature film financed. The money would be promised and then pulled back at the last moment so many times that I felt like a yo-yo going back and forth from so many movie financiers with the project I had written. After two years of documentaries, but no progress on my feature, I happened to see a movie called *Bank Job* starring George C. Scott. It was a light hearted bank heist story where five robbers lead by Scott steal a trailer (that has a safe in it) and haul it out into the hills. A safecracker 'expert' that was introduced to them enters the scene to crack the safe.

The expert first tries opening the combination lock with his ear to the safe door. Cut. He tries it using a stethoscope. Cut. He hits the door seam with chisel and hammer. Cut. He uses a drill. Cut. The robbers back off as he brings in acid to put into the seams of the safe. Cut. The now disappointed robbers are standing back as he uses a small explosive. Cut. The now bored robbers are hiding behind a desk as a larger explosive is used. Cut. Everyone is lying under protective blankets as even a larger explosive is used. When the smoke clears the safe is still not opened and the robbers look at each other and shake their heads about this so-called 'expert'.

"All right," the safecracker yells at the robbers. He moves into a super tight close-up, his face a fist of frustrated determination. "Everybody get out. I'm going to make me an ATOM BOMB."

Well, that character's frustration was exactly what I was feeling. At that moment I said to myself, "I'm going to make me an atom bomb, too." This became my mantra to rewrite my script even better, study cinema technique even harder, add more exciting characters to my screenplay and more importantly I added a much larger budget to support much larger production values and actors.

If I was ever going to get the money to make my movie I would make it my biggest and best, even if it was to be my last (it wasn't). I would be satisfied to have just this one movie made.

So I put everything I knew, felt, and had the skill for into the screenplay and production plan. I even decided to play a supporting part and do some stunts that I had fantasized about doing. This decision turned out to be one of the most rewarding things of making that movie. By the way, I was almost talked out of doing it (because "it will be too difficult to act and direct at the same time"). A trusted friend said that to me just two days before the beginning of filming. I got scared and planned to get someone else to play my part. Thank God it was too late to find another actor, so I was stuck with me in it. Even now when I show that movie that's the most fun for my new friends, to see me in it doing my own stunts.

Once again, don't let anyone talk you out of your dreams. That was the last time someone almost did.

Now back to the movie *Bank Job*. The expert runs outside the trailer and joins the robbers behind a rock.

The powerful explosion blows the trailer roof and walls away and as the smoke clears the safe is still there and closed. Then slowly, the door swings open. The robbers give out a cheer, but they soon stop as they see the trailer start to roll down the hill. The robbers give chase to their hard-earned money, still having to pursue it.

A perfect parallel to getting your big break. You spend all that effort trying to get your chance and then what happens? A lot more work comes as you try to accomplish what you first set out to do.

As far as my third feature film went, after studying for three months with success teacher Anthony Norvell in LA, I returned to San Francisco and in three days had my first investor for my movie. Two months later I was directing what would turn out to be my best movie, *Weapons of Death*.

Six weeks later I was finished. The money for post-production took a year to trickle in as I did the editing. But the movie was finished and later broke a house attendance record in a New York theater. A dubious distinction because on the bottom of the double bill (playing second to my movie) was the second run of *For Your Eyes Only*. I'm still wondering which movie drew in the crowds. Maybe you have an idea which movie was the larger draw.

So in business, get better, be prepared for your opportunities, and then work with focus and efficiency when they come.

16

UPGRADING YOUR IMAGE

Image has been mentioned all through this book—self-image and your image with other people. For some, image is not an important thing. Such as, "I'm a slob and I don't care who knows it." Better still I recently saw a young American man walking the streets of Tokyo wearing a T-shirt that read: "Life is not trying to look like a Calvin Klein ad." He must have taken great pains to dress down to prove his point. There is nothing wrong with him dressing like that or wearing that T-shirt. In fact, I kind of admire the style of it. But we are here to talk about the James Bond type of lifestyle, so a more stylish professional image is what we're going for. This is not found so much in clothes or looks, but in actions. A man is defined by his actions, his words, his accomplishments and his benefit to others. What kind of image do you want to have from now on? What lengths will you go to in correcting, expanding and presenting that image for business and personal relationships?

John Wayne, Self Reliance and Image

If we may for a moment examine another icon, there is

something special we can learn from him. In the movie *Rio Bravo* hired gun Ricky Nelson notices Sheriff John Wayne's rifle.

Ricky: "You always keep that carbine cocked?"

John: "Only when I carry it."

Ricky: "Why do you carry a rifle?"

John: "I found there were those that were faster with a handgun than me."

In those four lines we see that John Wayne is prepared by having his rifle always cocked, and that he knows his limitations and has compensated for them.

In that movie, the sheriff played by Wayne wants to be totally self reliant, and for the most part is. But it's his friends that come to his aid when he needs help. The idea of being prepared and finding a way to make up for your limitations is a serious one to consider.

While we're on the subject of John Wayne, look at how he forged an image for himself. He changed his name from Marion Morrison, learned his famous walk from actor Paul Fix, the sheriff of *The Rifleman*, and his acting style from Harry Carey Sr. He then carefully chose his movie parts to mould a consistent image, and started his own production company to have control of his image and product. This was a well thought out plan of image creation. Burt Reynolds said, "John Wayne worked hard at being John Wayne." Charlton Heston said, "The greatest thing that John Wayne ever did was to turn himself into a legend."

Think about this as we further consider our image. No,

we are not movie stars, true. But everyone has an image, like it or not, in business and with loved ones. Presenting the image that you want should be taken seriously, particularly when it comes to self-image. Your self-image becomes your belief in yourself. Your belief system (your subconscious emotional self) sets your actions and choices into motion, attracting or repelling success, money, relationships, health and enjoyment of life.

Upgrade Your Image Using The Power Of Three

Changing your image shouldn't be so instant that others think you are putting on a show or 'trying too hard' or have gone in for a fad that will soon wane. A three-month time period, like a season, should be used to gradually move into your new image, whatever that image may be. Some aspects of your image are easy to upgrade: a clean apartment (if you used to have a cluttered one); a more generous nature (if you used to be stingy); more open in your communication (if you used to be guarded); a more stylish appearance (if you used to be sloppy) and so on.

Other image aspects such as obtaining a new apartment, car, job, circle of friends and going on a Bond like vacation, will take more time and energy, especially financial energy. Increased skills such as learning a language or other educational growth also take more time and continued determination.

Using the 'power of three' will upgrade your image to others and yourself in different areas of your life. Simply explained the power of three is this: Upgrade three things in your life in a short period of time (about six weeks) and you will be perceived to have a stronger image.

Most Hollywood actors agents know that if they can

have their clients in three projects at about the same time it creates the image that they are 'hot' and 'happening'. For example, if an actor has a popular movie out, just had his autobiography published and won an award, people will take notice and think, "This guy is moving up."

You can upgrade and re-energize your relationship with your girl by doing three things within six weeks, like take her on a trip, have a birthday party for her and then take her to a concert to see her favorite performer. Do these things subtly and naturally (not like you planned to put all three together).

Always remember the power of three accomplishments in a short time period. Use it when you see an opportunity coming where you have a possibility of two accomplishments coming up. At that time try to work in a third within the same six weeks. Pull it off and you're catapulted up to the next level of image.

If the idea of image enhancement is too abstract for you to grab a hold of (and it is rather abstract), then just follow the upcoming 21 rules and your image will take a perceivable jump upwards in a few weeks.

RULES OF THE JAMES BOND LIFESTYLE

1. I never run out of cash.
2. I accomplish, learn, give and enjoy something every day.
3. My base of operations is always clean.
4. For challenges I improvise, adapt and overcome.
5. I dress up, even at home alone.
6. I eat fruit, vegetables, drink water and sleep.
7. I carry enough cash and credit to operate efficiently.
8. I chose my contacts carefully and avoid villains.
9. I never give up, but I can change directions.
10. I'm not afraid to pay for what I want.
11. I get good value for my time and money.
12. I circulate all things good. The bad stops with me.
13. Everyone I meet benefits from the experience.
14. I am always early for meetings.
15. I edit out negative verbalizations.

16. On the job, I'm always professional.
17. I am constantly learning by reading a book a week.
18. I tip freely like Bond.
19. My car is filled up, clean and ready to go.
20. I rent what I need and take mental possession of it.
21. I never run out of cash.

You'll find these rules on my web site on the "00 Agents" page where you can print them out and sign it like a contract. After you do, put it near your mission control space and follow them everyday. You'll soon see big changes in your lifestyle. Some that you've created yourself directly. Others that seemed to have come out of thin air like magic. These magical changes will be an indirect result of your actions that have accumulated while you were doing other things. Then at the right moment this 'progressive jackpot' will pay off for you unexpectedly. Go ahead and accept these 'bonuses'. You earned them by your good actions and by being serious about upgrading your life.

The most important thing about these unexpected benefits is that they will make you hungry for more, so you'll be inspired to take further action.

18

CLEARING THE SUBCONSCIOUS

To program the subconscious mind positively, it is beneficial to have it cleaned or 'cleared' first. You can replace dirty water with clean water by continuously pouring in the clean. But a more efficient way of doing it is to dump out the dirty water, clean the glass and then put in clean water. The subconscious works in the same way.

The following hypnosis/meditation session is very powerful, if done correctly. To do it correctly just means that you have to do the mental work of imagining the negative people or experiences that you want to release. This 'work' can be fun and satisfying, but it is work. You can't just sit or lie there meditating. You have to become an active participant.

The first part of this hypnosis session is relaxing the body to an almost sleeping state. The second part is doing the actual clearing by visualizing what and who you want to release, putting white cleaning light around that image, and letting it fly into space as you release the experience or forgive the person.

The next step is to forgive yourself and release the mistakes that you may have made. After that you visualize the experience that you want to have, seeing its completion in your mind and experiencing the joy of having it come into your life. From there you will gently and slowly come back to full awareness.

What I've done with this system is combine two similar hypnosis/mediation techniques together to make it very powerful. I've had amazing results using this technique in just a few days, even though I didn't think that I had any 'problems', bad experiences or people to release. But then they came up while I was in the hypnotized state. Here's how I was introduced to this subconscious clearing technique.

I went to a prosperity seminar in order to learn how to raise money for my next movie. That was the only reason I went. But in order to raise up my mind for higher sums of money I found out that I needed to clear my subconscious of my limited money beliefs. Studying with my first teacher, Anthony Norvell, made me recognize this right away. Norvell had guided me through prosperity meditations that were very powerful, but did not have a clearing the subconscious type of meditation. My next teacher, Marc Reymont, did.

In Reymont's class, after doing a hypnosis session, I got a tape version of it and did it daily at home for a week. Even though, like I said, I didn't have any real problems, I still had a few things to release and needed to be more non-reactive to certain situations that would frustrate me. I also needed to eliminate shyness in social situations. The meditations that I did at my home using my copy of this tape quickly did the trick. It felt like a miracle had happened.

Here's an example of what I experienced. I already mentioned the first feature film I did was in black and white, making it impossible to sell without a star actor and larger production values. And yes, I was swayed to do it in black and while because of the Kurosawa movies. Marc Reymont also said that I had put a mental limitation on my budget, thinking that I could not raise enough to make it in color. That was very true. Now five years had passed and I had finished two other features that were successful, but still I was having problems getting to the next feature and the next step. Hence, my continued interest in prosperity and human potential subjects, via books and seminars.

Although I wasn't too aware of it, every time I thought of my first black and white movie (*Drawn Swords*) I would cringe, make a face, groan and then shake my head quickly trying to escape the images of the financial and personal problems that came with that failure. Well, it's easy to see that an emotional reaction like that is bound to block needed belief energy. This was one of the things that had to be released. There was also an ex-partner on that project that had caused nothing but problems and the image of his face in my mind also made me shudder, even though I hadn't seen him in five years. I then realized that he needed to be released.

I also had to forgive myself for deciding to make the film in the worthless black and white. I hadn't realized that I blamed myself for that mistake because I was blaming everything on that bad partner. Marc Reymont also taught me that, "You are a hundred percent responsible for everything that you have attracted into your life, good or bad. It is your mental imaging, emotional belief and personal choices that got you into that experience."

This idea is what a lot of people don't want to hear. Which is why they stay away from anything that sounds like 'self help', 'time management' or 'motivational seminars'. They'd rather take a pass, blame someone or something on their lack of success and buy a lottery ticket.

However, I understood and agreed with everything my teacher was saying. So I was ready for his hypnosis/meditation sessions and did the best imaging, releasing and forgiving that I could because I really wanted to move up to the next level of my career and finances. I was still paying off the debts incurred from that first feature and I needed badly to rise above them.

So now I present this hypnosis session to you. You won't find this in any other place, as my teacher made his transition into the next world without leaving a book or published tapes.

Back Pain Disappears

Of course, any time you have any physical problem, SEE A MEDICAL DOCTOR FIRST. Then the hypnosis/meditation session can aid the body in its healing. But sometimes the pain can be psychosomatic, caused by the person himself.

Here's a true story of a person I was counseling. It's important that you read this so as to understand the potential power of this hypnosis session. Even with the success I've had with it, this experience impressed me.

I was counseling a twenty-nine-year-old woman on her career as a speaker in Tokyo, when she mentioned that she had continuous back pains. I asked her if she had fallen down or hit her back. She said she hadn't and had checked it out with a doctor and he couldn't find anything wrong. Then I asked her when it had started and she said three months earlier. After asking her a few more questions it turned out that the pain started when her art gallery had been damaged by the famous Kobe earthquake three months earlier, at which time her five partners/friends betrayed her and sold the gallery that she had wanted to keep going. The back pain had started from that time and continued in Tokyo where she decided to move, to escape her ex-friends.

The timing of her back pain with the betrayal of her friends was too much of a coincidence to be ignored. So I asked her if she would like me to put her into a hypnotized state, to release the negative emotions that she was most likely still mentally holding onto concerning that incident. She agreed. I first wrote down the names of her five ex-friends so I could have her release each one separately. She then gave me her small tape recorder to record the session with so that she could repeat it at her home as I advised her to do. She then did a good releasing when she was under hypnosis, forgiving and releasing each ex-friend one by one and then forgiving herself.

I saw her a week later. She told me that for some reason the tape recorder had not recorded the session so she couldn't do it at home. But the one session she had done in my office had been enough to stop her back ache one hundred percent. Checking with her a few months later, her back ache had gone for good, never returning after that first and only session. As a bonus, her speaking career had prospered.

This shows the effectiveness of this mediation as well as the power our minds have to block our success and even cause pain to our bodies.

So do a good job of releasing and forgiving when you use this meditation.

The Hypnosis/Meditation Session

I will make this available on tape in the near future on my web site on the 'Equipment' page. But until then you can use it here by reading it (or having a trusted friend read it) into a tape recorder and then following the instructions on the tape. It should be read slowly with a calming tone of voice and plenty of pauses between ideas. Start here:

Get comfortable in your chair with your hands on your lap. If you are lying down at home, get comfortable with your hands resting at your sides.

Begin by taking three deep cleansing breaths into your nose and out your mouth ... one ... two ... three ... Now gently close your eyes ... I want you to picture in your mind that you have an unlimited source of relaxation energy that is hovering over your head and it begins to slowly move down on to your head, relaxing the top of it ... now it moves down your forehead relaxing it ... now down to your eyes ... relaxing your eyes ... slowly close your eyes ... slowly close your eyes ... all tension is draining away ... draining away ... this relaxation now moves down to your cheeks and nose ... relaxing them ... the tension in your face is draining away ... flowing down and out of your face as this relaxation moves down to your mouth and chin and relaxes them ... all tension is draining away from your entire face ... relax ... relax ... relax...

Now your relaxation energy is flowing gently and slowly down your neck ... all the tension in the front and back of your neck is draining away ... draining away ... and you feel so relaxed ... so comfortable ... so easy ... your relaxation energy is now moving down your shoulders ... all tension in your shoulders is draining away ... draining away ... now the relaxation continues down your arms ... all the way down to your hands and fingers ... relax your arms ... your hands ... your fingers ... all the tension in them is running out down to the floor and draining away ... and you feel so good that you don't even want to move a muscle ...

that's right ... your don't even want to move a muscle ...

This relaxation energy now moves down to the large muscles of your chest and relaxes them ... relax and breath easy ... now down to your stomach ... relax ... relax ... all tension is going ... and even the sounds inside the room and outside the room are all contributing to your sense of relaxation ... that's right, even the sounds inside the room and outside the room are all contributing to your sense of relaxation ... your relaxation energy now moves down to your hips and thighs and legs ... relax your legs ... all tension in your legs is running out of them and onto the floor so that no tension remains ... only relaxation remains ...

You feel like you're floating on a cloud of relaxation ... drifting on a sea of relaxation ... you feel so good that you don't even want to move a muscle ... your body feels so wonderfully heavy ... your arms are comfortably heavy ... your legs feel so heavy so relaxed now, that you don't even want to move a muscle ...

Now in your mind you see an escalator in front of you that is going down to a very deep and wonderfully relaxing place ... the down escalator seems so inviting that you approach it ... put your feet on the first step ... your hand on the hand rail and start to go down ... down ... down ... and you feel so safe and secure ... you feel so relaxed as down ... down ... down ... you go...

While you are descending this wonderful escalator, I'm going to count backwards from 10 to 1 ... and as I do you will go deeper into your relaxation ... deeper than before ... it is like you are asleep ... but you are not asleep ... you are still listening to the sound of my voice and following my suggestions ... and you feel so good following my suggestions ... 10 ... 9 ... 8 ... 7 ... 6 ... deeper than before ... deeper than before ... 5 ... 4 ... relax ... 3 ... 2 ... 1 ...

Now you approach the bottom of the escalator and you

step off ... in front of you are two large beautiful carved wooden doors ... they look so nice and inviting that you push open these wooden doors and on the other side you see a green forest with a small river running though it ... the grass is green and thick and feels so good on your bare feet ... yes, your feet are bare and the cool grass feels so good as you walk though this wonderful forest ... you can hear the birds singing ... you can hear the small river water flowing ... and you feel so relaxed and comfortable in this special place of yours ... and up ahead you see two large trees with a hammock strung between them ... a soft comfortable hammock that looks so inviting that you walk over and lie down ... as you look above you can see the tall trees and the blue sky ... and now you can hear and feel a nice cooling breeze coming through the forest as you relax deeper than before ...

I'm going to count from five to one, and as I do you will go deeper into relaxation than before ... but you will still be listening to the sound of my voice and following the suggestions I make ... five ... relax ... four ... relax deeper than before ... three ... relax deeper than before ... two ... one ... you are now feeling so comfortable and so relaxed that you are ready to clear away anything that might hold you back from doing the things that you want to accomplish ...

Take one bad experience that happened to you. remember the people in that experience that have disappointed or angered you ... see that experience again ... see that experience again ... now feel bad about it one last time ... feel that bad experience one last time ... get angry at that person one last time ... now relax ... relax from that experience ... now imagine glowing white cleansing light around that person and experience ... see the beautiful bright, white love energy surrounding and soaking through the image of that experience or person ... and now with the white love light surrounding that experience ... release it now ... release that person now ... let it go ... let them go ... .see that image getting smaller and smaller ... flying up into space ... up into the stars ... getting smaller and smaller with the white love light energy surrounding it ... release it now ... give it to God now ... give it to space now ... forgive them now ... they can never hurt you, disappoint you, anger you again ... that's right ... they can never hurt you, anger you or disappoint you again ... release them now ... (twenty seconds of quiet) ...

Take a deep breath and blow out the last of your frustration ... the last of your anger ... the last of your disappointment ... breath in through your nose deeply ... and gently and slowly blow out your disappointment out of you mouth now ... release them now ... the bad energy is gone now ...

Now is the time to remember the mistakes of that situation or the mistakes you made with that person ... or the mistakes of being associated with that person ... and now is the time to forgive yourself ... forgive yourself for those mistakes ... you made those mistakes ... but now those mistakes are over ... forgive yourself now ... release yourself from those mistakes now ... you learned what you needed to learn, so forgive yourself now ... (twenty seconds of quiet) ...

Now is the time to visualize the accomplishment of your next mission, goal, or dream ... see it now ... see yourself at the very moment that you accomplish your dream ... feel that experience now ... live in that experience now ... (twenty seconds of quiet) ...

Now visualize a bright white cleansing light flowing through your body ... making you healthy and energetic ... that light is inside your body and projects outside ... just as if you were a bright light bulb ... shining bright with health energy ... hold the imagination of that white light in your body getting brighter and brighter ... giving you unlimited health ... (twenty seconds of quiet) ...

Now let the bright light relax and settle back into your healthy body ... let the light relax and return inside your healthy body ...

Now take a deep breath into your nose ... and slowly blow it out of your mouth ... now it's time to get up from the hammock ... and you feel so good and light as you get up ... walk across the forest to the two large wooden doors that are open and leading to the up escalator ... put you feet on the first step of the escalator, your hand on the handrail, and start to go up ... as you go up you slowly start to wake up from this wonderful successful meditation ... I will count from one to ten and as I reach ten you will be at the top of the escalator and totally awake, refreshed and energized ... one ... two ... you are starting to wake up ... going up the escalator ... three ... four ... you begin to move your fingers ... five ... six ... you begin to slowly move your arms ... seven ... eight ... you slowly open your eyes ... going to the top of the escalator ... nine ... ten ... your eyes are open and you are totally awake and refreshed ... Stretch out your arms and take a deep breath in through your nose, and be mindful of your final deep exhalation ... you are now completely awake and refreshed ...

End session

Every time that you do this session you should take a different problem, experience or person to your meditative level with you to release and forgive. Once you have done this for a week or so, you can use this same meditation to program in the goals that you want to achieve. Live in that successful experience for a few moments and work up emotional energy as you visualize yourself at the very moment of achieving your goal. This will deeply program the event, or accomplishment, that you want to experience so that your subconscious will help guide you to the action that you should take to bring that experience into physical manifestation.

Remember the key here is to start taking strategic action, even small steps, toward your goal. Meditation and visualization, even though very powerful, are not enough. You must go into action to bring about your goal.

19

THE GREATEST ADVENTURE

What's the greatest adventure that you can think off? Climbing the Alps up to Piz Gloria, the restaurant where *OHMSS* was filmed? Speedboating around Scaramonga's island in Phuket? Hang gliding over Nassau? Well, those come close. But I know that you'll find the greatest adventure in life to be self-change. To plan a goal, a dream, a fantasy, an accomplishment and then to see it through to fruition has to be the greatest adventure. This is because you are gathering up your own powers and bringing something into being that you at first might have thought impossible, and then there it is in front of you. Created by you. When you see yourself with it, you will also see that you have become a greater person. A person who has found his own powers.

Janet Leigh said of Dean Martin who came out of his post Jerry Lewis slump with *The Young Lions*, "I saw the man emerge. I saw the confidence come like 'Hey, I can do that'."

And when you "do that" your confidence will certainly come. You'll be hungry for the next step, the next challenge. Hungry to create the next experience. But be forewarned to enjoy, savor and record each experience in your mind and feelings.

Bruce Willis said, "In my twenties, I just went from experience to experience, without paying attention. And now I want my twenties back."

He could have benefited from the words that Frank Sinatra inscribed on his daughter Nancy's St. Christopher medal, "Be aware." Sinatra would always say, "To be aware is the number one priority."

Don't Back Slide

You might be jazzed up about moving forward in your lifestyle now after we've spent this time together and that's great. But be sure to keep up the energy throughout the months that follow. Get your Bond symbols, set up your base of operations, follow as many of the techniques here that you can. And if you start to back slide, it's okay. Take a few days off. Veg out in front of the tube and when you're ready, put on your Bond music CD and start cleaning up while Tom Jones is telling you to "strike like thunder ball," Shirley Bassey says you're the "man with the Midas touch" or Lulu tells you about "his million dollar skill."

That's the beauty of this kind of teaching. If you fall back for a week or two or even a month or two you can get back in action instantly.

But why fall back? Sure it will get tough climbing up the mountain. When it rains, pitch a tent and wait it out. When the sun is shining, run up that mountain while the good weather lasts.

For Your Eyes Only

I suggest that you initially keep this book and your new

actions top secret. This way your mind is not short-circuited by statements like, "What's this you're reading? What? Do you think you can be James Bond, just by doing the stuff in this book?"

Of course, the answer would be, "I'm not going to be James Bond, I'm going to be me, living the lifestyle that I want." But why answer it at all? Just gradually and naturally let people see the positive and productive changes in your lifestyle. Then if someone sincerely asks you what you've been doing to bring about this exciting upgrading of your lifestyle, you can mention the techniques you learned in this book.

Identify Your Target

Just by changing the word "kill" to "succeed" M's statement to Bond in *OHMSS* goes like this: "Your license to succeed is useless, unless you're able to identify your target."

Likewise, the information in this book and your personal power are useless without goals to use them on. I suggest you chose three goals right away. A small one (like clean up and organize your apartment), a big one (like a trip to Las Vegas or DisneyWorld), and a fantasy experience (like enjoying the *Dr. No* waterfall with your Bond girl). Then start to work on them. 'Work' being the operative word. Again, it can be fun and exciting work. It can be your greatest adventure.

You Are Living

Every time you face a challenge and ask yourself, "What would James Bond do?" Every time you stop in the middle of your mission and say, "I'm alive and this moment is fantastic." Every time this happens, you are living the James Bond lifestyle.